Raising Capable Kids

The Ultimate Guide to Chores, Character, and Confidence

By Faith Rachelle

ISBN: 978-1-0690664-1-1

I dedicate this book to all the parents who face the daily challenge of inspiring their children to become helpful, respectful, and capable individuals.
Your unwavering commitment shapes their future, which is essential for our future!
You can do it!

Please consider leaving a review,
as it helps Amazon Algaithim to get it to more families!
Thank you, and enjoy the book!

Guide to Unlocking Your Child's Complete Potential

Guide to Unlocking Your Child's Complete Potential

Parenting is a road filled with delight, laughter, and challenges. Let's be honest: times of total anarchy are certain. From planning extracurricular events and school schedules to ensuring everyone gets a relatively balanced meal, it may seem like we are constantly juggling. Many of us have a persistent question: "Am I raising my child to be capable of having the required skills for adult life?"

We all want our children to be confident, responsible, and kind people who can face life's obstacles with grace, perseverance, and resilience. However, with all of the commotion of modern parenting, it is easy to lose track of how to get there. This book is here to help. What's the secret? Chores.

Yes, that's right. Chores, also known as tasks.

I grew up with "Chores." Doing chores often came with a struggle, as there was discipline for not doing them. As an adult, I have found a new perspective on the tasks my parents asked me to do. Children, when hearing the word, sometimes become defensive. If we change our language with our children, it can be a bonding opportunity. For example, explain to your child that it would be helpful for them to do theirs as you are working on your tasks. That way, you are able to spend more time together.

Although asking your five-year-old to make their bed or asking your teen to assist with dishes seems like just another chore on an already heavy to-do list, these little tasks have great weight. Routine helps children to develop the skills and values required for lifetime success. Children learn from tasks how to take ownership, support the family, and grow to become strong problem solvers.

Still, there is more to it than assigning tasks and hoping for the best. This book is not about turning your house into an endless chore schedule. Rather, it is about redefining your—and your child's—view of chores as boring tasks to ones that offer chances for development. It is about fostering in every member, regardless of age, a family culture of cooperation, responsibility, and mutual respect whereby each makes a major contribution.

Chapter 1

Building Strong Kids Through Responsibility: The Power of Tasks

As parents, we want what is best for our kids. We envision them as becoming strong, capable, and confident people who tackle life's challenges with resilience.

So, how can we help them build these qualities? Interestingly, one of the best ways to do this is by tackling everyday chores, aka tasks, around the house. Tasks are actually a lot more critical for your child's growth and character development than you probably realize.

When children are given responsibilities, no matter how small, they learn valuable life lessons about accountability, responsibility, and teamwork. By contributing to the family, they begin to understand the importance of being part of a community that thrives when everyone plays their part. Research has shown that children who consistently participate in household tasks tend to exhibit greater self-control, emotional intelligence, and responsibility (Rossmann, 2014).

Beyond these qualities, however, tasks also offer children a sense of accomplishment. When they complete a task, they experience a moment of pride, and this feeling contributes to their self-worth. Over time, these small successes build a foundation of confidence that will carry them through more significant challenges in life.

How Responsibility Leads to Self-Confidence

Responsibility isn't just about getting things done—it is about building character. One of the most impactful lessons kids learn from tasks is that they are capable. They begin to understand that their actions matter and can make a difference, even if it's something as small as helping clear the table after dinner, putting their shoes in a designated spot or hanging up a towel when finished. These small steps will, when they are young, become habits.

One of the most impactful lessons kids learn from tasks is that they are capable.

Psychologically, when kids complete tasks, they activate their brain's reward system, specifically triggering the release of dopamine, a neurotransmitter that makes them feel good. Over time, as they complete tasks and receive praise or acknowledgment, they start associating the completion of responsibilities with positive feelings, building self-confidence and motivation (Graybiel, 2008).

Overcoming Common Doubts About Household Tasks

One common concern many parents have is whether assigning tasks might be too burdensome or even unfair. After all, we want our children to have carefree, enjoyable childhoods and not to feel overwhelmed by household responsibilities. It's essential to remember that the goal isn't to overwork your child but to help them develop essential life skills.

Another worry some parents face is that their children will resist or complain. This is perfectly normal—children, like adults, may not always feel enthusiastic about tasks. However, with consistency and encouragement, children can learn to see the value in their responsibilities. Plus, once they get the hang of it, they often surprise us with their ability to rise to the occasion. Children begin to acquire self-confidence and believe that they are trustworthy members of the family when given the opportunity to participate in activities and take on responsibility during their childhood. Giving children the opportunity to take on responsibilities and participate in activities leads to this development.

We can use possessing a sense of competence as a factor that contributes to developing both of these attributes to cultivate healthy and balanced self-esteem. Developing a sense of self-worth can accomplish this. When children successfully complete their assignments, they gain first-hand experience of how their activities impact their surroundings. The fact that they can do this gives them a sense of fulfillment and accomplishment.

Numerous studies lend credibility to the hypothesis that children trusted with duties at a young age have a stronger sense of self-worth and are more confident in other aspects of life, such as school and social interactions. These studies provide evidence that supports the theory that this does, indeed, occur. Research suggests that trusting younger children with responsibilities enhances their sense of self-worth compared to those without such trust. Dr. Jim Taylor, an expert in child psychology, conducted one of these investigations.

What is the significance of starting at a young age when it comes to developing habits that will last a lifetime? I am curious as to the reasons behind this.

When parents encourage their children to undertake chores at a young age, it helps them create habits that will remain with them throughout their entire lives.

These habits will continue to be passed down from generation to generation. Parents can assist their children in the process of acquiring habits by encouraging and modelling, creating routines that will last a lifetime. The early introduction of obligations not only aids in the development of responsibility but also helps to instill discipline and regularity in the individual over time. This is what makes the early introduction of responsibilities so beneficial. Since this is the case, it is beneficial to initiate obligations at an early stage of growth.

As they grow older and assume more responsibility on their own, this naturally becomes a part of them—a trait that they often carry into adulthood. When they leave, these young people will take their lifelong work ethic with them. The Grant Study at Harvard University revealed that young individuals who were required to carry out responsibilities as children had a greater chance of becoming successful and independent adults.

Many parents hesitate to delegate tasks to their children, fearing opposition or the possibility that their children will perform the tasks in a way that adds to their workload rather than being beneficial. These concerns may be the root of their anxiety. **Please keep in mind that children will only achieve perfection in their tasks after a period of time**, and the learning process is just as important as the outcome.

Understand this. Dr. Carol Dweck's research on the growth mindset suggests that difficulties are opportunities for learning. The findings may lead to this conclusion. Parents can assist their children in developing resiliency and cultivating motivation to improve themselves by supporting them as they navigate the earliest hurdles they encounter.

In Real Life:

In a cheerful suburban neighborhood, there lived a bright and spirited 10-year-old girl named Sophia. With a head full of dreams and a heart full of creativity, she loved painting, writing stories, and imagining worlds far beyond her cozy little home. However, when it came to household responsibilities, Sophia was less enthusiastic. Cleaning her room felt like an uphill battle, and helping with dishes? Forget about it! Her parents, Mark and Emma, knew it was time for a change.

One evening, after a particularly long discussion about Sophia's reluctance to help out, Mark and Emma gathered the family in the kitchen. They presented an idea that would soon transform not just their dinner routine, but also Sophia's attitude toward responsibility. "We're going to create a family task chart!" Emma announced with a smile.

"What's that?" Sophia asked, curiosity sparking in her eyes. "It's a way for each of us to contribute to our home," Mark explained. "We'll list out tasks, and each person can choose what they want to help with. You'll have ownership over your tasks, and we can work together as a family!"

Sophia was intrigued, but the thought of being responsible for anything still felt daunting. Nevertheless, she agreed to give it a try. After some discussion, it was decided that Sophia would set the dinner table each night.

At first, she approached the task with a sigh, dragging her feet as she walked to the dining room. Each evening, she would lay out the utensils and plates, her mind wandering to the adventures she could be having instead. But as the weeks passed, something began to shift in Sophia.

One night, as she placed the last fork down, she noticed her family gathering around the table, laughing and chatting excitedly. It dawned on her that she played a part in creating that warm atmosphere. Inspired, Sophia began to add her own personal touches to the dinner table. She started folding napkins into neat shapes—some nights, they resembled little boats, while other times, they were elegant fans.

Her parents noticed her growing enthusiasm. "Sophia, the table looks wonderful! I love the napkin boats!" Emma praised one evening, beaming with pride. Sophia's cheeks flushed with happiness; the acknowledgment made her feel important and valued.

As her confidence blossomed, Sophia began to take greater ownership of her responsibilities. She no longer saw setting the table as a chore but as an opportunity to showcase her creativity. On days when she felt particularly inspired, she would even add fresh flowers from the garden, making each dinner a special occasion.

One Friday night, Sophia had a brilliant idea. "Can we have a theme dinner?" she asked. "I can set the table with a pirate theme!" Mark and Emma exchanged amused glances but nodded in agreement. That night, the dinner table was adorned with a treasure map as the centerpiece, and the napkins became pirate flags. As they sat down to enjoy the meal, laughter filled the air, creating memories that would last a lifetime.

As Sophia continued to embrace her responsibility, her parents observed other positive changes in her behaviour. The once messy room that had often been a battleground of clothes and toys became more organized. With a newfound sense of pride, she began to take the initiative to tidy up after herself.

Her success with setting the table led to an unexpected ripple effect. Sophia started to realize that her contributions mattered and that being part of a family meant working together. This understanding deepened her connections with her parents and created an atmosphere of cooperation in the household.

One afternoon, after finishing her homework, Sophia surprised her parents by offering to help with the dishes. "I want to contribute more!" she said with a grin. Mark and Emma could hardly contain their excitement as they rushed to the kitchen, ready to tackle the task as a team.

In those moments of washing dishes together, they engaged in conversations about Sophia's day at school, her dreams for the future, and even her latest creative projects. The task that once felt like a chore had morphed into cherished family time, all sparked by Sophia's initial task of setting the table.

Practical Tips

Create a task chart.
Using a visual aid, such as a task chart, helps children see their progress. Rewarding them with stickers or points for completed tasks can motivate them to stay consistent.

Set clear expectations.
Explain the importance of each task and how it benefits the family. Clear expectations help children understand the value of their work, making them more willing to participate.

Incorporate fun
Turn tasks into games or challenges to make them more engaging. This is particularly useful for younger kids.

Conclusion

Incorporating tasks into your child's daily routine means more than just getting help around the house. It is an investment in their personal growth and development. By assigning meaningful responsibilities, you are helping your child build essential life skills like time management, responsibility, and independence. When learned early, these lessons set the foundation for future success, both at home and in the world beyond.

Reflection Questions

How was I raised in regard to doing tasks?

Was it a positive or negative experience?

What are my beliefs, and how do they affect my child?

Notes:

____
____
____
____
____
____
____
____
____
____
____
____
____
____
____
____

"Train up a child in the way he should go, and when he is old, he will not depart from it." - Luke 16:10

Chapter 2

Age-Appropriate Tasks: Setting Kids Up for Success

One of the most significant gifts we can give our children is responsibility. Like any gift, it needs to come at the right time, in the right way. Matching tasks to your child's age and developmental stage is essential for ensuring success. It's about setting them up for small wins and gradually building their confidence and competence. In this chapter, we will explore how to align the tasks you assign with your child's abilities and how to encourage growth through responsibilities that challenge them—but don't overwhelm them.

For example, toddlers love doing tasks that require them to classify and organize items, such as putting spoons in a drawer or putting their toys away. Setting the table or working in the garden becomes more complex as older children mature into school-aged children. On the other hand, adolescents can independently manage minor household tasks, such as preparing a small meal or doing their own laundry. It is crucial to ensure that the activities are appropriate for the child's physical and mental capabilities at each level to promote a sense of accomplishment and development.

The Right Tasks at the Right Time: How to Guide Your Kids Through Their Stages

Kids go through many different stages as they grow up, and these stages affect how ready they are to handle various responsibilities. Timing plays a key role when it comes to assigning tasks. For instance, it is a bit much to expect toddlers to handle a vacuum cleaner, but they might have fun helping out by wiping surfaces with a towel. Just like older kids can handle simple chores like sweeping or taking out the trash, younger ones need those tasks to be split into smaller, more manageable steps so they can feel a sense of achievement.

Kids between the ages of 2 and 5 are good at picking up on things and mimicking what they see around them. Kids enjoy copying their parents because it makes them feel proud. It is fantastic to see them get involved by helping with folding towels, sorting laundry, or even pulling weeds in the yard.

Once kids reach elementary school, typically between the **ages of 6 and 10,** they are ready to take on more structured responsibilities. Having your child keep their room tidy, taking the dog for a walk with you, or getting your lunch ready are all excellent ways to build skills like consistency and time management.

Kids aged 11 to 13 can start getting involved in meal planning, but it's good to have some supervision while they do it. Why not ask them to whip up a family meal once a week? You can help them pick out a healthy recipe and gather all the ingredients they'll need. Involving them in the process helps them feel responsible and promotes thoughtful decision-making. Along with meal planning, they can start making simple dishes like scrambled eggs or pasta. This will help them build their confidence in the kitchen and pick up some essential cooking skills.

As children advance to middle school, they are prepared to assume increasingly important responsibilities, which significantly contributes to their increased independence and self-assurance. Now is a great moment to give them the guidance they need while helping with tasks requiring a bit more planning and organization.

Right now, we can start giving out tasks, like managing the family's recycling efforts, to help them understand why taking care of the environment and getting involved in the community matters. On collection days, kids might sort recyclables and take the containers to the curb.

Middle school is an ideal time to encourage children to manage their schoolwork independently. Encourage them to keep track of their homework, projects, and extracurricular activities using a calendar or planner. This helps them develop organizational skills that will benefit them as they grow older.

When your kids get to high school, they are capable of starting to take on more grown-up responsibilities. **When they hit around 14 to 17**, they can handle tasks that not only help your home run more smoothly but also prepare them for life on their own.

A significant responsibility for high schoolers is to keep track of the family schedule. They can handle managing appointments, extracurricular activities, and even family events. It is an excellent way for them to improve their time management skills. A family calendar app or a big wall calendar could help keep everyone updated on what's happening during the week. Once they feel at ease, they can give everyone a nudge about those important dates—like that dentist appointment you might overlook—or help map out the weekend around different plans. It is a straightforward and effective method for teens to gain a sense of control while managing their responsibilities.

Teens can definitely start tackling more advanced tasks when it comes to yard care. They might have already mowed the lawn, but now they can pick up some skills for caring for the entire yard—like raking leaves, trimming hedges, or even using a power washer to clean the driveway. These tasks let them feel proud about keeping the home tidy and give them some practical experience with tools they will use when they have their own place someday. Seasonal chores are a great way to get everyone involved—whether it's shovelling snow in the winter or prepping the garden in the spring, these tasks offer perfect chances to learn some valuable life skills.

Taking care of your car is really important. Teens can begin picking up some basic skills—like checking tire pressure, refilling the windshield washer fluid, or even giving the car a good vacuuming. These little tasks might look minor, but they contribute to grasping what it takes to maintain a vehicle. Honestly, it's a fantastic way to prepare for when they get their own car to take care of.

In terms of home maintenance, older teens can take on tasks like mowing the lawn, organizing the garage, or helping with minor repairs around the house. They should also be involved in more complex chores, such as painting a room or assembling furniture, which prepares them for independent living.

In addition to shopping, high schoolers should be capable of preparing full meals for the family once or twice a week. By this stage, they can manage multiple elements of a meal, such as cooking a main dish while preparing sides or salads, with minimal supervision. They also learn how to coordinate timing in the kitchen, ensuring all parts of the meal are ready simultaneously—an essential life skill.

Another key responsibility for this age group is budgeting. Teaching teens how to create and manage a simple budget, whether for family groceries or their personal allowance, helps them develop an understanding of money management. This can include tracking spending, saving for future purchases, or even opening their first bank account.

Lastly, it's a perfect opportunity for your teens to step up and take on a leadership role in the family. Why not suggest they lend a hand to their younger siblings with homework or chores? It could be a great way to bond! It's not only about getting some extra support; it's also about letting your teen step up as a role model and build those leadership skills. Also, it boosts their confidence to be the one people turn to for advice and guidance.

What is important is that as your child grows, the tasks should also evolve, ensuring continuous learning and growth.

The American Academy of Pediatrics suggests that children who are given developmentally appropriate tasks tend to develop better problem-solving skills and a stronger sense of autonomy.

When children successfully complete a task, their brain releases dopamine, reinforcing positive behaviour and building motivation (Graybiel, 2008). This not only gives them a sense of accomplishment but also instills a love for helping out, as they associate tasks with feelings of success and contribution.

Encouraging Growth Through Achievable Responsibilities

Responsibility should never feel like a punishment but rather an opportunity for growth. Encouraging children to participate in household tasks gives them a sense of ownership. It allows them to feel like they are contributing to something larger than themselves—the entire family's well-being. When children succeed in their tasks, no matter how small, they feel a sense of accomplishment that builds self-esteem and encourages further growth. This success is critical as children navigate developmental stages filled with new challenges.

The tasks assigned should always feel achievable, but it's okay to push the boundaries of what your child can do.

This encourages resilience and a growth mindset, viewing challenges as opportunities rather than obstacles.
It encourages resilience and a growth mindset, viewing challenges as opportunities rather than obstacles.
Encourages resilience and a growth mindset, viewing challenges as opportunities rather than obstacles.

For example, instead of giving preschoolers the simple task of setting the table, provide them with the challenge of organizing different items like plates, forks, and napkins, allowing them to think critically and develop sorting skills.

As they grow older, introduce more responsibilities, like preparing a simple snack or taking out the trash, ensuring that the tasks remain within reach but encourage skill-building.

In Real Life:

One sunny Saturday morning, after a busy week of play and exploration, Sarah decided it was time to give Emma a special "job" of her own. "How about we sort the socks together after laundry day?" she suggested, her eyes sparkling with excitement.

Emma's face lit up. "Can I really help?" she asked, her voice filled with enthusiasm.

"Of course! You can be my sock-sorting assistant!" Sarah replied, kneeling down to meet her daughter's gaze. "It'll be fun, and I'll show you how."

As they gathered the freshly laundered socks, Sarah set up a little station on the living room floor. She demonstrated how to match the socks, explaining that they would take it one pair at a time. "Just find two that look the same and put them together," she instructed gently. "If you get stuck, just ask for help!"

At first, Emma was a little overwhelmed. The colorful array of socks seemed to blur together, and she often mixed up pairs, giggling at her mistakes but also feeling a hint of frustration. "I can't do it, Mommy!" she exclaimed, her little hands clutching a mismatched sock.

With a soft smile, Sarah reassured her, "That's okay, Emma! We're learning together. Let's take a deep breath and try again. Remember, we're just looking for one pair at a time."

Encouraged by her mother's patience and support, Emma took a deep breath and focused on the task. Gradually, she began to grasp the concept of matching socks. With every correct pair she found, a sense of pride bubbled up inside her. "Look, Mommy! I did it!" she squealed, holding up two identical pink socks with glee.

As the weeks went by, Emma's sock-sorting skills improved tremendously. The once daunting task transformed into a fun game she looked forward to. Not only was she sorting socks, but she also began to enjoy helping her parents with other household tasks. One day, after successfully matching socks, Emma proudly declared, "Can I help with folding the towels, too?"

Sarah and Tom exchanged glances, their hearts swelling with pride. "Absolutely, sweetheart! We'd love your help!" they said in unison, thrilled to see their daughter's willingness to contribute.

With each small win, Emma was not just sorting socks—she was building a foundation for responsibility, independence, and confidence. Her parents understood that these seemingly simple tasks were crucial for her development. By providing her with manageable responsibilities that matched her abilities, they nurtured her growth in ways they had yet to fully appreciate.

As the family continued their Saturday routine, Emma began to take initiative. She would wake up each Saturday morning, excited to help with the laundry, already thinking about the fun she would have sorting socks and folding towels. Her parents delighted in watching her transformation, knowing that they were teaching her valuable life skills that would serve her well in the future.

Reflecting on the power of small wins, Sarah and Tom realized that their approach was fostering more than just household responsibility; it was instilling a sense of pride in Emma. The joy she found in her contributions was contagious, spreading throughout their family and creating a warm atmosphere of cooperation and teamwork.

As Emma grew, her confidence blossomed into a strong sense of responsibility. The lessons learned through those early tasks paved the way for her future endeavors. Whether it was helping with school projects, organizing her room, or even taking care of her younger siblings, Emma embraced her roles with enthusiasm and commitment.

Practical Tips

Start with small, manageable tasks that fit your child's age and ability.

Toddlers (ages 2-3): Put toys in a bin and put clothes in the laundry basket.

Preschoolers (ages 4-5): Helping set the table, feeding pets, organizing books.

Elementary schoolers (ages 6-9): Make their bed, clear the table, and sweep small areas.

Pre-teens (ages 10-12): Washing dishes, helping with meal preparation, taking out the trash.

Conclusion

Assigning age-appropriate tasks isn't just about getting household help—it's about preparing children for success in life. By matching responsibilities to their abilities and gradually increasing the complexity, parents help their children develop confidence, resilience, and valuable life skills. Starting early and continuing through the teenage years ensures that these skills are deeply ingrained, leading to capable, independent adults.

Reflection Questions

What are some simple tasks I can assign to my child that match their developmental stage?

How do you handle situations when your child struggles with a task that might be too challenging?

How can I gradually increase the complexity of their tasks to foster growth and learning?

Chapter 3

Instilling Values While Keeping the House Tidy

Keeping a clean home isn't just about maintaining order and appearance—it's a powerful opportunity to teach our kids essential values. When you invite children to join in with daily household tasks, you're not just getting help with the laundry or dishes. You're actively shaping their character, teaching them the value of teamwork, patience, and self-discipline, all while building a solid family foundation. Often, without the kids realizing it, the household transforms into a mini-classroom where they learn valuable life lessons.

Using Tasks to Teach Core Values

Let's start with **discipline**. Consistently following through with daily tasks requires a level of self-discipline that may not come naturally to every child. However, with time and guidance, kids can develop this skill. Research shows that routines help children develop the prefrontal cortex, the area of the brain responsible for executive functions such as planning, decision-making, and self-control (Diamond, 2013). The more consistent they are with completing tasks, the stronger these executive functions become, leading to better self-regulation and focus. Asking children to tidy up their rooms or clean up after themselves teaches them more than just how to maintain a tidy space. They're practicing **self-control**.

Think about it: They might prefer to keep playing with their toys or watching TV, but choosing to stop and finish their task teaches them how to manage their impulses. In a world full of distractions, learning to focus and complete a task from start to finish is an essential skill that will benefit them as they grow into adulthood.

For example, imagine you've asked your eight-year-old to tidy their room every evening. Initially, it may feel like a constant battle, but over time, you'll notice they start doing it without as much resistance. Why? Because they've learned to follow a routine and develop self-discipline, which gradually becomes part of their natural behaviour. That's the beauty of instilling discipline through daily tasks— eventually, it becomes second nature. You just need to stick with it!

How Tasks Nurture Empathy and Patience

Empathy is another essential value that can be taught through shared household duties. When kids help out at home, they start to see how their contributions benefit the whole family. This understanding fosters a sense of empathy as they realize that their actions make a difference. According to developmental psychology, empathy begins to emerge in early childhood but continues to develop through adolescence (Eisenberg et al., 2006). By involving kids in tasks that help others, like setting the dinner table or folding laundry, they begin to understand the concept of teamwork and the value of contributing to a group.

For instance, let's say your child helps you fold laundry. Maybe they're folding their clothes, but they also have to fold their siblings or household towels.

In this small act, they are developing empathy.

They are beginning to understand that their actions affect others and that their help can make a difference. This is especially true when the task benefits someone else, like helping set the table for dinner or making the bed for a family member who is running late. These little acts foster a sense of care and compassion, which are at the core of empathy.

Consider a scenario where you have your older child help their younger sibling with picking up toys. Not only does this teach responsibility, but it also fosters empathy. The older child learns to appreciate how their younger sibling may struggle with tasks that are easy for them, encouraging patience and compassion.

From a psychological perspective, teaching children to care for others through tasks activates the **mirror neurons** in their brains, which are crucial for understanding the emotions and intentions of others (Rizzolatti & Craighero, 2004). This neurological process encourages empathy by allowing children to "mirror" the experiences of those around them. So, when they perform a task that benefits someone else, such as helping a sibling, they're not just performing a chore—they're learning how to step into someone else's shoes, a skill that will benefit them in all aspects of life.

Building Family Foundations Through Shared Tasks

When your whole family comes together to share responsibilities around the house, you're doing more than just keeping things tidy. You are creating a sense of togetherness that builds a strong family foundation. Family systems theory suggests that when families work together on common goals, they foster stronger emotional bonds and resilience (Minuchin, 1974). Tasks aren't just about getting the house clean; they are about working together as a team, strengthening relationships, and building trust. Take the Johnson family, for example. Every Saturday morning, they gather to tidy up the house. Every family member has their own jobs, like dusting and vacuuming, but they always team up in the same rooms, swapping jokes and stories while they clean. As time went on, these moments became more about the feeling of togetherness than the actual chores. It brought the family closer together and showed the kids that working as a team can turn even the simplest tasks into something fun.

These shared moments also release **oxytocin**, the "bonding hormone" that strengthens relationships and creates a sense of security and connection (Carter, 2014, *pp. 65, 17–39*). Working together towards a common goal activates this system, making the family feel more united and emotionally close.

Let's say you and your children spend a Saturday morning cleaning the house together. Instead of everyone working separately, you decide to make it a team effort. You clean the living room while your kids help by dusting and vacuuming. Maybe you turn on some music and turn it into a fun family activity. At the end of the day, the house is clean, and everyone feels a sense of accomplishment. More importantly, your kids have learned the value of teamwork and the satisfaction that comes from contributing to a shared goal.

In Real Life:

In a bustling household, the evening routine often revolved around one central theme: dinner. For 12-year-old Jake, the kitchen was a place of mystery and wonder, a realm where his parents created delicious meals while he hovered nearby, usually absorbed in his own world of video games and homework. Jake had never been asked to step into this culinary domain, and he was perfectly fine with that—until one fateful evening changed everything.

It was a typical Wednesday when Jake's parents decided it was time for a change. With their busy schedules and the onset of a new school semester, they realized they needed to involve Jake more in household tasks. That evening, as they gathered in the living room, Jake's mom announced, "Jake, tonight you're going to help make dinner. How about you try preparing a simple pasta dish?"

Jake's initial reaction was a mix of surprise and apprehension. "Me? Cook? I've never done that before," he stammered, his face reflecting uncertainty.

"Don't worry! We'll guide you through it," his dad reassured him, pulling out a simple recipe for spaghetti aglio e olio. The ingredients were minimal: pasta, garlic, olive oil, and a sprinkle of parsley.

With a hesitant heart, Jake ventured into the kitchen, where he found the ingredients neatly laid out on the counter. Following his parents' step-by-step instructions, he began the process of cooking. At first, every task felt daunting. Boiling water seemed like an uphill battle, and chopping garlic required a level of finesse he wasn't sure he possessed.

But with each passing moment, Jake's confidence grew. His parents cheered him on from the sidelines, offering tips and encouragement. As the pasta cooked, the enticing aroma filled the air, sparking a sense of pride within him. After a little over half an hour, the dish was ready. Jake plated the spaghetti, garnishing it with a sprig of parsley, and called his family to the table.

As they gathered around, Jake's heart raced with anticipation. He watched as his parents took their first bites, their faces lighting up with delight. "This is amazing, Jake! You did a fantastic job!" his mom exclaimed, her eyes shining with pride.

To Jake's astonishment, the simple dish he had prepared was not just edible but genuinely delicious. The meal was accompanied by laughter and compliments, turning the dinner into a celebration of his achievement. For the first time, Jake felt a sense of ownership and pride in contributing to the family's mealtime.

Encouraged by his success, Jake's newfound interest in cooking flourished. He began volunteering to help with other meals, experimenting with new recipes and flavors. Over the next few weeks, he planned family dinners, surprising his parents with tacos, stir-fry, and even homemade pizza. Each meal brought with it laughter, bonding, and a sense of accomplishment that invigorated the family dynamic.

But the impact of this culinary adventure extended beyond just the kitchen. Jake's parents noticed significant changes in his behaviour and approach to responsibilities. With his cooking duties came a newfound sense of organization. He began to apply the same step-by-step approach to his schoolwork, breaking tasks into manageable parts and prioritizing his assignments. The chaos of his homework routine transformed into a more focused and deliberate effort.

Jake's gradual journey toward independence began with a simple task in the kitchen, but it grew into a life lesson that reached far beyond cooking. He learned the value of responsibility, the importance of following through on tasks, and the joy of creating something meaningful.

Through his culinary adventures, Jake not only developed a valuable life skill but also strengthened the bonds with his family. This experience taught him that stepping out of his comfort zone could lead to unexpected joys and personal growth, setting the stage for a future filled with resilience and confidence.

Jake's story serves as a reminder to parents and children alike: sometimes, all it takes is a single opportunity for independence to spark a journey of growth and connection.

Practical Tips

Model the behaviour you want to see: Children often learn best by observing. When you approach your tasks with patience and care, your kids are more likely to follow suit.

Focus on effort, not just results: Instead of only praising a completed task, celebrate the effort and teamwork that went into it. This reinforces the importance of being involved and persevering through challenges.

Incorporate tasks into family time: Turn shared responsibilities into bonding opportunities. Whether it's cooking together or cleaning up as a team, make it an enjoyable part of your family routine.

Conclusion:

Daily tasks go beyond just tidying up the house—they are a chance to teach your kids meaningful values. When you teach kids **self-control, empathy, patience, and teamwork** through everyday chores, you are helping them build the skills they will need to grow into caring, responsible adults. When your family comes together to share responsibilities, you are not just creating a tidy and organized home; you are also strengthening your family bonds and connections.

Reflection Questions

How can you use household tasks to teach empathy and patience?

42

What family tasks could become shared activities to build teamwork and cooperation?

Remember a moment when your family came together to tackle a task. How did it change things for your family?

"*And whatever you do, do it heartily, as to the Lord and not to men.*"
- Colossians 3:23 (NKJV)

Chapter 4

Creating a Task System That Works for Your Family

When it comes to managing household tasks, one of the biggest challenges parents face is creating a system that actually works. Sure, it's easy to make a list of what needs to be done, but how do you transform that list into a routine your family can follow without feeling overwhelmed or overworked? This chapter is all about finding that sweet spot—where tasks get done consistently, and no one feels like they're drowning in responsibilities.

Let's be honest:

Keeping up with household duties can sometimes feel like trying to keep your head above water. Some weeks, everything runs smoothly, and other weeks—well, let's just say the laundry piles up faster than you can fold it. The goal here isn't perfection. Instead, it's about setting up a balanced task system that works for your family, helps build long-lasting habits, and allows everyone a bit of breathing room.

How to Set Up a Balanced, Easy-to-Follow Household Routine

When you think about setting up a task system, what comes to mind? Maybe it's a chore chart on the fridge, a dry-erase board filled with daily duties, or even a list of assignments posted by each child's room. Whatever you imagine, the key is creating a system that fits into your family's busy schedule while teaching responsibility.

The first rule of thumb is to start small. If you're introducing tasks to your kids, avoid overloading them with too much at once. Start with just one or two simple tasks per family member. Research shows that small, manageable changes are less stressful, especially for children who may resist new routines if they feel overwhelmed (Dweck, 2006). When kids succeed in completing small tasks, it boosts their confidence and encourages them to take on more responsibility over time.

Consistency is also critical. Once tasks are assigned, stick to them. Routines help children feel more secure because they know what is expected of them and when. The brain's prefrontal cortex, which governs decision-making and planning, thrives on routines, improving a child's time management and organizational skills (Golinkoff & Hirsh-Pasek, 2016).

However, while consistency is essential, so is flexibility. Life doesn't always go according to plan, and trying to rigidly enforce a system when things go wrong can lead to frustration. A system that allows for adjustments—like swapping out tasks when schedules get hectic—reduces stress and makes the routine more sustainable in the long term. Families that balance structure with flexibility are more likely to maintain their task routines (Taylor, 2013).

Let's look at how one family made this work. Jennifer and her two daughters, Ella (8) and Grace (11), struggled to keep up with daily cleaning tasks. Jennifer initially tried to assign each daughter a strict list of daily duties. After a few weeks, it became clear that the rigid system wasn't working—tasks were missed, and everyone was frustrated. So, Jennifer decided to start smaller. She assigned each girl just one or two tasks and introduced **"swap days,"** allowing them to trade duties or take a break when their schedules got hectic. This simple change helped the family stick to their routine and improved household cooperation.

Finding the balance between structure and flexibility is vital to creating a task system that genuinely works.

Tools to Make Tracking Tasks Simple and Fun

Tracking tasks doesn't have to be tedious. With a bit of creativity, you can make it a fun and motivating experience for everyone in the family. One classic and effective tool is the task chart. Task charts offer a visual way for kids to see their responsibilities and track their progress. Younger kids might enjoy using stickers to mark off completed tasks, while older kids might prefer using a checklist they can mark or erase when their duties are done.

For tech-savvy families, there are apps that help you organize household tasks. Using apps makes it easier for families who are always on the go to stay connected to the task system.

The important thing is to choose a method that fits your family's lifestyle, whether it's a paper chart, an app, or even a simple whiteboard. The system should be easy to follow and flexible enough to adapt when things get busy.

In Real Life:

As the school year began, Jessica and Mark found themselves overwhelmed with the daily demands of work, homework, and household responsibilities. They noticed their home often felt chaotic, with tasks piling up and the children reluctant to help. Frustrated by the lack of cooperation, they realized it was time for a change. They needed a chore system that would not only lighten their workload but also teach Lily and Ethan the value of contributing to the family.

Jessica and Mark began by holding a family meeting to discuss their vision for a new chore system. They emphasized the importance of teamwork and how everyone could play a role in maintaining a tidy home. Together, they identified the daily and weekly chores needed to keep their household running smoothly, such as:

- **Daily Chores:** Make beds, set the table, feed the pets, and tidy up toys.
- **Weekly Chores:** Vacuuming, dusting, taking out the trash, and cleaning the bathroom.

To ensure the system was easy to follow, Jessica and Mark decided to assign chores based on age-appropriateness. Lily, being older, would take on more responsibility, while Ethan's chores would be simpler and manageable. They created a color-coded chore chart that displayed each family member's responsibilities for the week, allowing for easy tracking.

While establishing the chore system, Jessica and Mark recognized the need for flexibility. They didn't want the kids to feel overwhelmed by rigid schedules. To strike this balance, they introduced a "Chore Card" system. Each chore was printed on a card, and Lily and Ethan could choose when to complete their assigned tasks within the week.

For example, if Lily had the chore of vacuuming, she could decide to do it on Wednesday or Saturday, depending on her homework load or extracurricular activities. This flexibility empowered the children to take ownership of their responsibilities while maintaining a sense of structure.

To make tracking chores engaging, the Phillips incorporated a reward system. For every completed chore, the kids earned "chore points," which they could redeem for fun family activities like movie nights, extra screen time, or a special outing. They created a colorful chore board in the kitchen that displayed each child's points, turning the chore tracking process into a friendly competition.

The family also took advantage of digital tools to enhance their chore system. They downloaded a family organization app that allowed them to set reminders, track completed chores, and celebrate achievements. The app sent notifications when a chore was due, making it easier for the kids to stay on track without feeling nagged.

After implementing their chore system, the Phillip family noticed significant improvements. Lily and Ethan became more proactive about their responsibilities, often reminding each other to complete their tasks. The sense of teamwork fostered a stronger family bond, with the kids even working together on chores like organizing their playroom.

Jessica and Mark were relieved to see a reduction in household chaos. The weekly chore chart provided clarity, and the flexibility of the Chore Card system allowed the kids to manage their schedules effectively. Moreover, the reward system motivated Lily and Ethan to take pride in their contributions, reinforcing positive behaviour.

The Phillip family's journey in creating a chore system illustrates the importance of balancing structure with flexibility. By involving the children in the process, setting clear expectations, and introducing engaging tools, Jessica and Mark cultivated an environment of responsibility and teamwork. This approach not only lightened their load but also empowered Lily and Ethan with essential life skills that would benefit them beyond the home.

As families strive to establish their chore systems, the Phillip family's experience serves as a valuable reminder: with a little creativity and collaboration, chores can transform from mundane tasks into meaningful opportunities for growth and connection.

Practical Tips

Use natural transitions: Assign tasks that fit into your child's daily routine, like tidying up after dinner or making their bed right after waking up. This minimizes resistance and creates a seamless flow from one activity to the next.

Create a task jar: Write various household tasks on slips of paper and place them in a jar. Each week, family members can draw their assignments, making it a fun way to distribute duties.

Build-in task breaks: If your family struggles with following routines, build in small breaks or "rest days" when kids can trade tasks or skip one small duty without consequences. This teaches flexibility while maintaining structure.

Conclusion:

We discovered the importance of teaching children about accountability and ownership through household tasks. Assigning age-appropriate responsibilities helps children develop self-discipline, fostering a sense of pride in their accomplishments. By integrating tasks into daily routines, parents create opportunities for children to learn about commitment and the positive outcomes of hard work. Ultimately, these lessons form the foundation for responsible adulthood, equipping kids with the skills they need to thrive in life.

Reflection Questions

How does your family currently handle household tasks?

What's working, and what's not?

Where could you introduce more flexibility into your current system without losing consistency?

What tools or systems could make tracking tasks more engaging and motivating for your kids?

Notes:

54

Chapter 5

Raising Motivated Helpers Without Bribes or Rewards

Motivating kids to take responsibility for their tasks without relying on bribes or rewards can feel like an uphill battle, can't it? You want them to take ownership, but it often seems like the only way to get them moving is to promise something in return. While rewards can be useful for short-term results, depending too heavily on them may hinder long-term growth. The key lies in building internal motivation, where kids want to help out because they understand the value of their actions—and feel good about doing them.

Raising motivated helpers requires a shift in focus from offering external rewards to fostering pride, accomplishment, and ownership. The goal isn't just getting things done. It's about helping children develop skills that carry into adulthood without expecting something in return every time. When kids only act for rewards, they miss out on the intrinsic satisfaction of knowing they've done a good job. Instead, tasks can become transactional, which weakens self-discipline over time (Deci & Ryan, 2000).

So, how do we make this shift from external rewards to internal motivation?

Moving Beyond Rewards: Inspiring Kids to Complete Tasks Because They Want To

It's tempting to use a reward system for chores or responsibilities, especially when it seems to get results. However, research shows that over time, this approach can undermine the natural drive to do something simply because it's the right thing to do or because it feels good. A study by Deci, Koestner, and Ryan (1999) demonstrated that external rewards can reduce intrinsic motivation, particularly if the task is one the child could enjoy or feel proud of. Rewards shift the focus from enjoying or taking pride in the activity itself to just obtaining the prize.

> _**Intrinsic motivation** is defined as doing an activity for its inherent satisfaction rather than for some external, unrelated reward._

One way to foster intrinsic motivation is by helping your children recognize the satisfaction that comes from completing a task well. After a child finishes cleaning their room, for example, instead of offering a reward, encourage them to take a moment to enjoy how tidy their space is. You can say, "Doesn't the room feel more peaceful now?" or "Look at how much better it feels in here!" This helps them connect their efforts with positive feelings, which are essential in building internal motivation.

Let's look at Harper, a 9-year-old who wasn't thrilled about helping around the house. Her parents initially incentivized her with stickers and extra screen time, which worked for a while. But soon, Harper started dragging her feet again—

unless those rewards were in play. So, her parents changed their approach, focusing on how Harper's efforts made the household run smoother and how good it feels to contribute. Over time, Harper started to take more pride in her tasks, and the need for constant rewards faded.

Research supports this approach. Studies have shown that focusing on the outcome and personal growth encourages children to stick with a task even when no immediate reward is involved. Grolnick and Kurowski (1999) found that children who are encouraged to reflect on their accomplishments and how their actions help others tend to develop a stronger sense of internal motivation.

Cultivating a Sense of Pride and Ownership in Responsibilities

Another key to building intrinsic motivation is giving kids a sense of ownership over their tasks. When children feel like they have control over what they're doing, they're more likely to invest effort and care into completing their responsibilities. The brain's reward system, particularly the release of dopamine, responds well to feelings of autonomy. Deci and Ryan (2000) found that when children are allowed to take control over how they manage their responsibilities, their satisfaction and motivation increase significantly.

So, instead of simply assigning tasks, try letting your kids choose from a set of household duties. This gives them some control and helps them feel invested in the process. Research by Grolnick (2003) shows that when children are involved in making decisions about their responsibilities, they are more likely to feel committed to following through. Additionally, using language that reinforces their ownership, such as, "Look how well you've organized your room!" rather than "I'm glad you cleaned your room," helps shift the focus from seeking parental approval to personal pride.

Let's take another example. Ethan, a 10-year-old, often felt like chores were forced upon him. His parents decided to let him choose when and how he would complete his responsibilities. They allowed him to plan his schedule and choose the order of tasks. The result? Ethan began to feel empowered and in control, which improved his motivation and willingness to help.

Positive Behaviour Reinforcement: Building Lasting Motivation

One of the best ways to support intrinsic motivation is through positive behavioural reinforcement. This technique emphasizes reinforcing desirable behaviour with positive feedback rather than material rewards. Psychologist B.F. Skinner, known for his work in behavioural psychology, demonstrated that reinforcing behaviour increases the likelihood of it being repeated. However, it's the type of reinforcement that matters.

Verbal reinforcement—like praise or positive feedback—can be particularly effective when building motivation in children. In a study conducted by Henderlong and Lepper (2002), researchers found that children who received praise for effort and progress (rather than just outcomes) showed more interest in and perseverance toward tasks over time.

Reinforcement should focus on the process: praising the effort, persistence, and strategies used to complete the task rather than just the final result.

For example, instead of saying, "Great job cleaning the kitchen," try, "I noticed how hard you worked to make sure everything was spotless—that kind of attention to detail really pays off." This type of feedback reinforces the importance of effort and instills a growth mindset (Dweck, 2006), where children learn that they can improve through persistence and hard work.

In Real Life:

In a vibrant household filled with the sounds of laughter and activity, the Ramirez family was navigating the ups and downs of daily life. With two children, Sofia (10) and Max (8), parents Clara and Miguel were determined to cultivate a sense of responsibility in their kids, especially when it came to household chores. However, they noticed a growing reliance on rewards to motivate their children to help around the house. Clara and Miguel wanted to raise motivated helpers without relying on bribes or extrinsic rewards.

Clara and Miguel had initially used a reward system to encourage Sofia and Max to complete their chores. Each time they finished a task, they earned stickers that could be traded for treats or outings. While this method brought short-term compliance, the parents realized it wasn't fostering genuine motivation or a sense of responsibility in their children. Instead, Sofia and Max were primarily focused on the rewards, naging their parents and not doing the tasks well.

Feeling frustrated, Clara and Miguel decided it was time to change their approach. They wanted their children to find intrinsic motivation and understand that their contributions were important to the family unit.

The Ramirez family held a family meeting to discuss their goals for household responsibilities. Clara and Miguel emphasized that chores were not just tasks but essential ways to contribute to the family's well-being. They wanted Sofia and Max to feel a sense of pride in their contributions and recognize the impact of their efforts on the home environment.

To foster this sense of ownership, Clara and Miguel introduced the concept of "family contributions." They explained that each chore they completed helped create a comfortable and enjoyable home. They also encouraged Sofia and Max to personalize their responsibilities. For example, Sofia chose to take charge of organizing the family game night, while Max expressed interest in watering the plants.

To further instill pride in their work, Clara and Miguel started a "Family Contribution Board" in the kitchen, where they displayed the children's completed chores along with a note of appreciation for their efforts. This visible acknowledgment helped the kids see the direct impact of their contributions.

As the Ramirez family continued to develop their chore system, Clara and Miguel focused on helping Sofia and Max internalize the value of helping others. They modeled this behaviour by sharing stories of how they felt fulfilled when they contributed to the family, whether by cooking dinner or helping with laundry. By connecting their actions to feelings of pride and satisfaction, they helped the children understand that their efforts had intrinsic value.

When Sofia and Max completed their chores, Clara and Miguel offered smart praise that highlighted the specific actions the children took. Instead of simply saying, "Great job!" they would say, "I really appreciate how you organized the game night! It made our evening together so much more fun." This type of recognition helped the children feel valued for their specific contributions and reinforced the idea that their hard work was appreciated.

Over time, Sofia and Max began to embrace their roles as motivated helpers without the need for external rewards. They started to take initiative in their chores, volunteering to help cook dinner, set the table, or tidy up the living room. With the focus on pride and ownership, they no longer viewed chores as burdensome tasks but as opportunities to contribute to the family's happiness.

The Family Contribution Board became a beloved part of their home. Sofia and Max enjoyed seeing their names listed next to completed chores and often collaborated on projects, celebrating each other's efforts. The environment shifted from one of obligation to one of teamwork and camaraderie.

Clara and Miguel were thrilled with the changes they observed in their children. Sofia and Max displayed increased confidence and self-esteem, and their sense of responsibility extended beyond chores to their schoolwork and friendships. They learned to appreciate the satisfaction that comes from working hard and contributing to something bigger than themselves.

The Ramirez family's journey in raising motivated helpers without relying on bribes or rewards showcases the power of intrinsic motivation. By fostering a sense of pride and ownership in their responsibilities, Clara and Miguel empowered Sofia and Max to see the value in their contributions.

Through smart praise and recognition, they cultivated an environment where the children felt appreciated and valued. As families seek to inspire their children to help around the house, the Ramirez experience serves as a valuable reminder: with a focus on internal motivation and a sense of belonging, chores can transform into meaningful opportunities for growth and connection, enriching family life and instilling lasting values.

Practical Tips

Let them take the lead: Give your child some control over when and how they complete their tasks within reasonable limits. Autonomy boosts motivation and makes children feel more in charge of their actions.

Praise effort, not just results: Focus on the effort and process your child uses rather than just the final outcome. This builds resilience and a positive attitude toward challenges.

Encourage task ownership: Involve your child in choosing their responsibilities. Ask them what tasks they feel capable of handling or what they'd like to take responsibility for, reinforcing their sense of control and autonomy.

Make contributions visible: Show your child how their efforts contribute to the well-being of the family. "The dishes you washed mean we can eat on clean dishes for dinner tonight. Thank you!" This makes the task purposeful and highlights their contribution to the household and how it affects events coming up.

Reflect on accomplishments: After a task is completed, encourage reflection. Ask your child how they feel about their work and how their efforts made a difference. This builds long-term motivation by connecting effort with positive outcomes.

Conclusion:

We explored the transformative power of fostering intrinsic motivation in children, moving beyond the use of bribes and rewards. By emphasizing the satisfaction and pride that come from completing tasks, parents can instill a more profound sense of ownership and responsibility in their children. This approach not only nurtures a love for contributing to the household but also lays the groundwork for strong self-discipline and perseverance as they grow into adulthood. Ultimately, cultivating internal motivation equips children with essential life skills that enable them to thrive in a world where external rewards are not always present.

Reflection Questions

When was the last time your child completed a task without expecting a reward? How did they respond?

How can you encourage your child to feel more ownership over their responsibilities?

What small changes can you make to focus more on the satisfaction of completing tasks rather than offering rewards?

"Finally, brethren, whatever things are true, whatever things are noble, whatever things are just, whatever things are pure, whatever things are lovely, whatever things are of good report, if there is any virtue and if there is anything praiseworthy–meditate on these things." – Philippians 4:8

Chapter 6

Turning Task Battles into Cooperation and Teamwork

Household tasks often feel like battlegrounds, especially when kids resist them. If you've ever found yourself in a stand-off over cleaning a room or putting away toys, you're not alone. Many parents face this challenge daily. But what if we could turn these battles into moments of cooperation? It's possible—and it might not be as hard as it seems. Let's explore why kids resist tasks and how to inspire teamwork instead of tension.

Why Do Kids Resist Tasks?

Children often resist tasks because they see them as interruptions to their playtime or something they "have to" do. This resistance isn't just about being stubborn—developmentally, kids, especially younger ones, struggle with impulse control and delayed gratification. The prefrontal cortex, which governs these executive functions, isn't fully developed until children reach their mid-20s (Diamond, 2013). So when you ask a child to stop what they're enjoying and start a chore, it can feel like an overwhelming request. Naturally, they resist.

Rather than seeing this resistance as defiance, try viewing it through a developmental lens. Understanding this can help you approach the situation with more patience and empathy. Instead of demanding immediate compliance, offer a transition period with tools like a five-minute warning before starting a new task. This simple strategy gives your child time to mentally shift from play to work, easing the transition.

Rather than seeing this resistance as defiance, try viewing it through a developmental lens.

From Power Struggles to Teamwork
Imagine this scenario: You ask your 7-year-old to tidy up their art supplies after a fun craft session. They groan, roll their eyes, and start complaining. It's tempting to dig in and demand they do it right away. But power struggles like this often escalate, leaving both of you frustrated.

Now, let's try a different approach. Instead of making it a "you vs. them" situation, invite them to work with you as a team. Say something like, "Let's tackle this together, and we'll be done in no time. I'll organize the markers while you gather the paper." Partnering with your child not only reduces the burden but also models cooperation. Working alongside them turns the task into a shared experience instead of a battle.

Psychologically, kids are more likely to engage positively when they feel they have a partner rather than an authority figure telling them what to do (Grusec & Goodnow, 1994). This approach fosters a sense of shared responsibility, encouraging a cooperative mindset.

Battle Strategies for Parents: Staying Calm When You've Hit Your Limit

As a parent, it's easy to feel overwhelmed when you're dealing with resistance day after day. It's common to hit your limit and feel frustration rising. When this happens, it's important to have strategies to calm down so that you can respond thoughtfully instead of reacting in the heat of the moment.

Creating a Spirit of Cooperation

A powerful way to foster cooperation is to let your child have a say in how tasks are done. Kids have a natural desire for autonomy, and research shows that giving them choices helps them feel more in control and more motivated to cooperate (Deci & Ryan, 2000). For example, you could say, "Do you want to clean up your toys before or after lunch?" Offering simple choices like this reduces resistance and helps your child feel empowered.

Example: Lisa used to struggle with her 8-year-old daughter, Mia, overfeeding the family dog. Instead of nagging, Lisa started offering Mia the choice to decide when to do it within a specific timeframe. Mia felt more in control, and the task shifted from being a dreaded chore to something she took pride in.

Turning Chores into Opportunities for Teamwork

Children thrive when they feel their contributions are valued. When they see how their efforts help the family, it builds a sense of belonging and teamwork. Instead of seeing chores as burdens, kids can begin to view them as opportunities to contribute.

Research shows that children who participate in family tasks develop a strong sense of community and cooperation (Whiting & Edwards, 1988). They also gain valuable life skills like problem-solving, time management, and perseverance.

The Developmental Benefits of Teamwork
Involving children in household tasks isn't just about getting things done—it's about building skills that will last a lifetime. When children help with tasks, they learn how to collaborate, take responsibility, and manage their time. Over time, these skills foster independence and help them develop a healthy sense of self-reliance.

Positive Behavioural Reinforcement
Positive reinforcement is vital to turning task resistance into cooperation. Studies on behavioural reinforcement show that children are more likely to repeat behaviours when they receive positive feedback (Skinner, 1938). Rather than focusing on the outcome, focus on the effort they put into the task.

For instance, instead of saying, "Good job cleaning up," try acknowledging their effort: "I noticed you worked really hard to organize your toys today." This type of specific praise reinforces their actions and encourages them to stay engaged in future tasks.

Here are a few battle-tested strategies to calm yourself and regain focus:

1. Take a Pause
When you feel your frustration bubbling over, give yourself

permission to pause. Tell your child, "I need a moment to think," and take a few deep breaths. I found that taking three slow, deep breaths, as we are told, is not as effective as **two fast, quick breaths with a slow release, which** is far more effective. Give it a try! Also, teaching your child **two fast, quick breaths with a slow release will help them regulate their amygdala, which will help calm them down.** This simple act can help regulate your nervous system, giving you the space to gather your thoughts before responding. You might even step out of the room for a moment to compose yourself.

2. Use Grounding Techniques
When you are feeling overwhelmed, grounding techniques can bring you back to the present moment and reduce feelings of frustration. A popular technique is the "5-4-3-2-1 method," which helps you focus on your senses:

Name five things you can see.
Name four things you can feel.
Name three things you can hear.
Name two things you can smell.
Name one thing you can taste.
This quick exercise shifts your focus from frustration to the present moment, helping you regain control of your emotions. It actually releases a chemical in your brain to bring you down.

3. Reframe the Situation
Sometimes, reframing how you think about the task can help ease frustration. Instead of viewing your child's resistance as defiance, try seeing it as an opportunity to

teach them skills like cooperation, responsibility, and problem-solving. Shifting your perspective can transform the moment from a battle into a teaching opportunity.

Example: Instead of thinking, "Why won't they just listen to me?" reframe it as, "How can I help them develop the skills to manage their tasks?" This mindset shift reduces feelings of frustration and helps you focus on long-term growth.

4. Create a Calming Phrase

Create a calming phrase that you can repeat. Something as simple as "I am calm; I can handle this" can help reset your mindset in stressful moments. Repeat it silently or out loud whenever you feel yourself getting close to your limit.

5. Set Realistic Expectations

Sometimes, the source of frustration is rooted in unrealistic expectations. Understand that children are still learning, and their resistance is not a reflection of your parenting. It is a normal part of their development. By setting realistic expectations, you can give yourself grace when things don't go perfectly.

In Real Life:

It was a typical Saturday morning at the Rodriguez household, and like clockwork, 5-year-old Oliver was resisting cleaning up his toy cars scattered across the living room floor. His mom, Maria, sighed as she prepared herself for yet another battle. This wasn't new—Oliver's groaning and stalling had become routine anytime cleaning up was mentioned. Maria often found herself getting frustrated, which usually led to tense stand-offs.

But today, Maria was determined to try something different. She had recently read about strategies to foster cooperation instead of conflict and she wanted to see if they could turn the tide in their favour.

Earlier that morning, Maria had almost fallen into the usual pattern of frustration. But she'd remembered a calming technique she had recently learned: the "two fast, quick breaths with a slow release." When Oliver first resisted, she'd taken a moment to step aside, breathe, and reset her mindset before approaching the situation.

By giving herself that brief pause, Maria had been able to stay calm and approach Oliver with patience and understanding, rather than reacting out of frustration.

Rather than demanding Oliver clean up immediately, Maria used a simple tool: transition time. She crouched down to Oliver's eye level and gently said, "Hey buddy, you've got five more minutes to play, and then we'll need to clean up the cars. How about I sing your favourite song when it's time?"

Oliver perked up at the mention of his favourite tune and nodded, feeling less ambushed by the request. The five-minute warning helped him mentally prepare for the shift from playtime to cleanup time.

When the time came, she decided to make it a team effort. "All right, let's work together. I'll pick up the cars by the couch, and you can gather the ones near the table," she suggested with a smile.

Working as a team made the task feel less like an order and more like a game. To her surprise, Oliver happily started gathering his cars, excited to see who could finish their section faster. They laughed together as they organized the toys into their bins, the tension that usually filled the air now replaced with cooperation.

Once the living room was clean, Maria knew it was important to praise the process, not just the outcome. Instead of the usual "Good job cleaning up," she said, "Wow, you stayed really focused while putting your cars away. I could see how hard you were working! Look how nice and tidy the living room looks now!"

Oliver beamed, clearly proud of himself. By acknowledging his effort, Maria reinforced the idea that it wasn't just about the task being done—it was about how he approached it.

Later that day, when it was time for Oliver to help set the table, Maria offered him a choice: "Would you like to put the plates out before or after we finish setting the napkins?" Giving him a say in how the task was done made Oliver feel more in control and, once again, reduced resistance.

With these simple shifts, Maria found that Oliver's attitude toward tasks was changing. Rather than battling over every little task, they were starting to work together as a team. Over time, the need for power struggles faded, replaced by a sense of cooperation and shared responsibility.

The Rodriguez family's story shows how powerful small changes can be when it comes to household tasks. By using transition times, turning chores into teamwork, offering choices, and focusing on effort, Maria found a way to reduce conflict and inspire cooperation. These strategies didn't just make chores aka tasks easier—they strengthened their bond as a family, teaching Oliver important life skills in the process.

Practical Tips

Approach tasks as a team: Work together with your child to show that tasks are a shared responsibility, not just something imposed on them.

Use transition times: Give your child a countdown or a five-minute warning before starting a task to ease the transition. I find singing a song to transition helps.

Take care of yourself: Use calming techniques like deep breathing, grounding exercises, or a short pause to reset before addressing your child.

Conclusion:

We delved into transforming household task battles into opportunities for cooperation and teamwork, emphasizing the developmental reasons behind children's resistance. By shifting our approach from authority to partnership, we empower children to take ownership of their responsibilities while fostering a sense of shared accomplishment. When children feel their contributions are valued, they develop essential life skills like collaboration, problem-solving, and time management that serve them well into adulthood. Ultimately, these strategies not only ease the tension around chores but also cultivate a family environment built on teamwork and mutual respect.

Reflection Questions

How does your child respond when asked to help with things around the house?

When you feel overwhelmed by your child's resistance, what strategies help you stay calm?

How could offering choices during tasks reduce tension and improve cooperation in your home?

What could you do to make household tasks feel more like teamwork rather than battles?

Notes:

"Behold, how good and how pleasant it is for brothers to dwell together in unity!"
- Psalm 133:1

Chapter 7

Leading by Example: How Your Actions Shape Your Child's Attitude

When it comes to teaching responsibility, your actions as a parent speak louder than words. Children are constantly watching and learning from the behaviours they see. Your approach to your responsibilities, whether calmly or with stress, with a positive mindset or reluctance, sets a powerful example for how they will approach theirs.

Research shows that observational learning, where children absorb behaviours from their caregivers, is one of the most fundamental ways children learn (Bandura, 1977). Whether you're aware of it or not, your children are constantly absorbing the way you handle daily tasks, stress, and responsibilities. So, how can you turn this natural tendency into a positive, shaping your child's attitude toward responsibility?

The Influence of Parental Actions

Imagine this: you are rushing to prepare dinner, feeling stressed and frustrated, muttering about how much there is to do. Not so hard to imagine! While you may be focused on getting things done, your child is picking up on your stress and learning that tasks like cooking or housework are something to resent.

Now, consider a different scenario. You're calm, working through the same dinner prep, but this time, you say, "Let's tackle this together so we can enjoy a family meal." By modelling a calm, proactive attitude, you're not only getting the task done—you are teaching your child that even mundane tasks can be approached with positivity and teamwork.

Children often mirror the actions and attitudes of their parents. Studies show that when parents model responsible behaviour, their children are more likely to adopt the same approach to tasks and responsibilities later in life (Vygotsky, 1978). This is why your example is one of the most powerful teaching tools you have.

In Real Life: Erin's Approach to Leading by Example Consider Erin, a single mom of two who constantly juggles work and household responsibilities. Instead of making chores a solo effort, she includes her kids in the tasks. Each weekend, she organizes a family cleaning day, assigning tasks according to their abilities. She folds laundry while her youngest picks up toys, and her oldest vacuums the living room.

Over time, her children began to internalize the value of these tasks. By working alongside their mom, they learned that responsibility is not just something that's told to them— it is something everyone participates in. They also saw how teamwork made the chores quicker and less daunting.

Erin's strategy not only fostered her children's sense of responsibility but also strengthened their bond as a family.

Rather than seeing chores as a punishment or inconvenience, her children view them as a shared task that keeps their home running smoothly. This modelling through participation encourages kids to adopt a positive attitude toward household tasks, making them more likely to take the initiative as they grow older.

Your example is one of the most powerful teaching tools you have.

Consistency Is Key:
How Actions Reinforce Long-Term Behaviour

When children consistently see their parents approach responsibilities with positivity and efficiency, they are more likely to adopt similar habits. It's not about being perfect—every parent has stressful days—but it is about creating an environment where handling responsibilities calmly and constructively is the norm.

Research suggests that children raised in homes where parents model responsible behaviour tend to develop stronger organizational skills, better time management, and more positive attitudes toward responsibility (Bronson & Merryman, 2009). Your behaviour sets the foundation for how they will handle tasks as they get older—whether it's schoolwork, helping at home, or even managing their own lives as adults.

Consistency, however, is crucial. Even during times of chaos, maintaining a calm demeanour or explaining why certain tasks need to be done helps reinforce the idea that responsibility is not a burden but a necessary part of life. This is especially important when life becomes overwhelming; it's in these moments that your children are paying the most attention to how you react.

Teaching Responsibility Beyond Chores
Responsibility goes beyond just getting chores done. It extends to life skills, time management, and handling stress. When you model how to manage bills, prepare for work deadlines, or plan family outings, you're teaching your child the broader concept of responsibility. These skills help children understand that being responsible is about planning, organizing, and following through with commitments.

For example, when you sit down to budget or plan out family activities, involve your children. Let them see the thought process that goes into organizing these tasks. You might explain why sticking to a budget allows you to save for a fun family trip or how organizing family schedules ensures that everyone's needs are met. This way, your children learn that responsibility has tangible benefits.

In Real Life:
9-year-old Emma was well-known for her stubborn refusal to help out around the house. Whether it was folding laundry or clearing the dinner table, Emma always seemed to find an excuse to avoid pitching in and made it difficult to even approach her. Her parents, David and Sofia, often found themselves caught in a cycle of frustration, trying to convince Emma to complete her tasks without a fight.

One evening, after yet another argument over cleaning her room, David and Sofia realized something important—they weren't leading by example as well as they could. They had been telling Emma what to do but weren't always modelling the behaviour themselves. It was time for a shift in their approach.

Step 1: Show, Don't Tell

Instead of just asking Emma to clean her room the next morning, Sofia decided to make a point of organizing the family's living room in front of her. She calmly picked up books and arranged the cushions on the couch, all without saying a word about chores. She wasn't doing it to lecture or to pressure Emma—just to show what responsibility looked like.

Curious, Emma wandered into the living room and watched her mom work. "Why are you cleaning up right now, Mom?" Emma asked.

Sofia smiled and said, "I like keeping things tidy so we can all enjoy the space. It makes me feel good when things are organized."

Her calm demeanor and positive attitude toward the task made an impression on Emma, who hadn't seen chores framed in such a light before.

Step 2: Invite Participation Without Pressure

Later that day, when David began cleaning up the yard, he casually invited Emma to join him: "I'm going to clean up the garden a bit before dinner. Want to help me water the plants?"

David's approach was relaxed—there was no demand, just an invitation. He didn't push when Emma hesitated, simply saying, "It'll be quicker if we do it together."

Emma, noticing her dad was doing the work anyway, decided to give it a try. As they worked side by side, David didn't lecture or talk about the importance of chores. Instead, they chatted about Emma's day at school, her favorite books, and the weekend plans. This teamwork, without pressure, began to show Emma that helping wasn't just about the task—it was an opportunity to connect.

Step 3: Model a Positive Attitude

Over the next week, David and Sofia continued to lead by example. They made an effort to talk about how much they enjoyed the sense of accomplishment that came from completing household tasks. Whether it was Sofia tidying the kitchen or David folding laundry, they both made a point to express satisfaction with a job well done.

Emma noticed how her parents didn't treat chores as burdens but as part of their daily routine. They weren't complaining or arguing over tasks; instead, they demonstrated a calm and positive attitude. Slowly, Emma's own attitude began to shift.

Step 4: Use Encouragement, Not Criticism

When Emma started helping out more, David and Sofia made sure to acknowledge her efforts. But rather than showering her with generic praise, they focused on specific aspects of her work. "Emma, I really liked how carefully you put the dishes away tonight," Sofia said after dinner one evening. "It makes a big difference when everyone helps out."

This kind of feedback reinforced Emma's behaviour, making her feel proud of her contribution without feeling like she was just being told what to do. The encouragement was genuine, tied to her actions, and made Emma more eager to help in the future.

Step 5: Consistency is Key

David and Sofia knew that leading by example wasn't a one-time fix. They committed to staying consistent with their actions and continuing to model the behaviour they wanted Emma to adopt. Each time they worked on a task, they invited Emma to join without pressure, showed her how they approached it calmly, and gave positive feedback when she participated.

Within a few weeks, Emma's resistance to chores had noticeably decreased. She began taking more initiative, offering to help set the table or fold her own clothes without being asked. The battles over tasks became fewer and farther between, replaced by a sense of teamwork and shared responsibility.

The Gonzalez family's experience highlights the power of leading by example. When David and Sofia shifted from simply telling Emma what to do to showing her how they handled their own responsibilities, Emma began to internalize the importance of helping out. Their calm, positive attitudes toward chores—combined with invitations to work together—helped foster a sense of cooperation without pressure.

Through consistency and encouragement, the Gonzalez family transformed the household dynamic, turning chores from a battleground into a shared experience of teamwork and connection. Emma learned that tasks weren't just obligations—they were opportunities to contribute to the family, just like her parents had modelled for her all along.

Practical Tips

Shaping Attitudes Through Example
Model Enthusiasm for Tasks: Children are highly attuned to your emotional tone. If you approach responsibilities with positivity, they're more likely to mirror that attitude.

Be Transparent about Adult Responsibilities: Share some of your responsibilities with your child in age-appropriate ways. Let them see that being responsible is part of adult life, too.

Turn Responsibility Into Fun: Use timers, create games, or offer small rewards to make responsibility feel less like a chore and more like a challenge to conquer.

Conclusion:

Here, we emphasized the profound impact parental actions have on shaping a child's attitude toward responsibility. By modelling a positive and proactive approach to daily tasks, parents can instill essential life skills in their children that extend beyond household chores. Erin's story illustrates how collaborative efforts can transform mundane tasks into opportunities for teamwork, reinforcing the notion that responsibility is a shared journey. Ultimately, consistent modelling of responsible behaviour not only fosters independence and initiative in children but also equips them with the skills needed to navigate their own lives with confidence and resilience.

Reflection Questions

How do you handle your responsibilities in front of your children?

 What messages might they be picking up from your behaviour?

What are some simple ways you could involve your child in daily tasks, helping them view responsibilities more positively?

How do you respond when tasks feel overwhelming?

____

____

____

____

____

____

____

____

____

____

____

____

____

____

____

"And be kind to one another, tenderhearted, forgiving one another,
even as God in Christ forgave you."
Ephesians 4:32

Chapter 8

The Power of Early Habits

Have you ever walked through a field of tall grass? The first time, it feels like you're battling the elements, trying to forge a path through the thick blades. But with each step you take, it gets a little easier. By the tenth time, you're gliding through effortlessly, having created a well-worn path. This is much like how habits work in our brains. Each time we repeat an action, we're reinforcing a neural pathway until it becomes second nature.

When it comes to our children, forming positive habits early can set them on a trajectory for lifelong success. Engaging in consistent, healthy routines helps kids internalize these practices, shaping their decision-making and self-control as they grow. It is never to late to start, no matter how old your children may be. In this chapter, we'll dive deep into how the habits formed in childhood—good and bad—impact responsibilities later in life. You might find it enlightening (and a bit empowering) to see just how pivotal these early years are in shaping responsible adults.

The Science Behind Habit Formation
Let's start with a little brain science, shall we? Neuroscientists have been studying how habits form and what they mean for our behaviours. Here's the gist: repeated actions strengthen neural connections in our brains, making

those behaviours feel automatic over time. So, when we teach our children to form positive habits, we're quite literally helping them build a roadmap in their minds that they can follow as they grow up.

At the heart of this process is a part of the brain called the **basal ganglia**, which is crucial for developing habits, recognizing patterns, and performing routine behaviours. What's fascinating is that when children engage in repetitive actions, their brains are highly receptive, allowing them to create strong neural pathways. This is a prime time for forming good habits—it's when their brains are like sponges, soaking up everything around them (Duhigg, 2012).

Understanding Habit Loops
To better grasp habit formation, let's explore the concept of **habit loops**. A habit loop consists of three components: the cue, the routine, and the reward.

1. **Cue**: This is the trigger that initiates the habit. For example, it might be a certain time of day, an event, or even an emotional state. If your child sees their toys scattered across the floor (the cue), they might feel prompted to clean up (the routine).
2. **Routine**: This is the behaviour itself. In our example, cleaning up the toys is the routine. It's the action taken after the cue has been recognized.
3. **Reward**: This is the positive reinforcement that follows the routine, encouraging the behaviour to be repeated. It could be a sense of accomplishment,

praise from a parent, or even just the satisfaction of seeing a clean room.

Understanding this loop can help parents craft effective strategies for habit formation. By ensuring that children have clear cues, engaging routines, and meaningful rewards, parents can guide them toward developing lasting positive habits.

How Early Habits Affect Responsibility in Adulthood

You might be wondering, "How do these early habits translate into adulthood?" Well, it's quite simple. When children are given age-appropriate tasks and responsibilities, they start to understand what it means to contribute to their families. This understanding is crucial for developing their sense of accountability, perseverance, and overall work ethic as they transition into adulthood.

For instance, think of a child who learns to manage their homework effectively. This isn't just about grades; it's about building the skills to handle various life demands. Similarly, if a child consistently helps around the house—whether it's putting away dishes or keeping their room tidy—they're naturally adopting behaviours that will serve them well as adults.

Research highlights that children who take on household responsibilities tend to develop self-regulation and executive functioning skills—traits linked to success later in life (Mischel, 2014). Essentially, you're setting them up for the kind of life where they can manage their time, set goals, and stick to commitments, which are crucial in both professional and personal realms.

Introduce Habit Stacking

Rather than just introducing new tasks or responsibilities, try linking them to habits your child already performs. This technique, known as "habit stacking," can be incredibly effective in helping children build new habits. For example, if your child already brushes their teeth every night, you could add the task of tidying their room right afterward. By associating the new action with an already established one, the process of habit formation feels more natural and automatic.

Focus on the "Why" Behind the Habit

Children are naturally curious, so use this to your advantage. Explain why certain habits are important rather than just expecting them to do something because they're told. For instance, instead of just asking them to clean up their toys, explain how it keeps their play area safe and makes it easier to find their toys next time. When children understand the reasoning behind their actions, they're more likely to internalize and maintain the habit.

Create Visual Cues

Visual aids can be very powerful in reinforcing habits. Consider using charts, checklists, or even fun drawings that act as reminders. For example, if you want your child to remember to wash their hands before dinner, a colorful sign near the sink can serve as a visual cue. Over time, they'll associate the visual reminder with the habit, and eventually, the behaviour will become second nature even without the cue.

Incorporate Habit Journaling

Introduce a simple habit journal where your child can track their progress. Not only does this make habit-building fun, but it also provides a visual representation of their consistency. As a parent, you can review their journal together, using it as a tool to celebrate accomplishments or discuss areas for improvement. This instills a sense of ownership in your child for their own habits and achievements.

The Power of Autonomy

Allow your child to have some autonomy in choosing which habits they want to form. While you'll provide guidance, giving them a sense of control can be empowering. For example, you could present a list of household responsibilities and let them pick which ones they'd like to take charge of. This approach encourages them to take ownership of their actions, which strengthens their commitment to forming the habit.

How Habits Shape Accountability

One of the most significant aspects of early habit formation is its impact on accountability. When kids regularly complete tasks or responsibilities, they learn the importance of following through on commitments. This skill becomes invaluable in adulthood, influencing work ethic and personal integrity.

For example, think about a child who consistently turns in their homework on time. They're not just learning academic skills; they're also developing the ability to meet deadlines and manage their time effectively. Fast forward to adulthood, and those same skills translate into being reliable at work, balancing personal commitments, and maintaining integrity in relationships.

Developing resilience is another critical benefit of this accountability. When children follow through on tasks—even when it's difficult—they cultivate perseverance. Adults who have learned this skill are better equipped to handle setbacks and remain committed to long-term goals.

In Real Life:

Meet Emily, a spirited 8-year-old with a passion for arts and crafts. From a young age, Emily's parents believed in the importance of instilling responsibility through small, manageable tasks. They understood that fostering a sense of accountability early on would set the foundation for her future success.

Starting Small: The Craft Bin

Emily's journey began with a simple task: organizing her craft bin. Her parents introduced this responsibility when she was just 5 years old. At first, it felt overwhelming to her. But they turned it into a fun game—each time Emily successfully sorted her colored pencils, stickers, and glitter into designated containers, she earned a small sticker on her chore chart. This visual representation of her progress motivated her to complete the task.

As she learned to manage her craft supplies, Emily's parents gradually increased her responsibilities. By age 7, she was also responsible for cleaning up after her art projects, which included putting away materials and wiping down the table. With every completed task, Emily gained a sense of accomplishment, and her self-esteem flourished.

A Turning Point: The School Project
Fast forward to Emily's 6th-grade science project. This time, the assignment was more complex: she had to create a model of the solar system. Emily remembered her previous experiences with responsibility and approached the project methodically.

She broke the project down into manageable tasks: researching the planets, gathering materials, constructing the model, and preparing her presentation. Instead of feeling overwhelmed, she felt empowered. The habits of organization and accountability she developed in her early years shone through, allowing her to manage her time effectively and create a well-executed project.
When it was time to present, Emily spoke confidently about her model, receiving high praise from her teacher and classmates. This experience not only solidified her love for science but also reinforced her belief in the importance of hard work and planning.

Adulthood: Navigating College and Beyond
As Emily transitioned into high school, she continued to build on the foundation laid by her parents. Her ability to manage time and responsibilities became even more critical as she juggled schoolwork, extracurricular activities, and a part-time job.

Emily thrived in this environment because she had developed effective study habits early on. She was adept at setting goals, prioritizing tasks, and following through—skills she had honed through those early responsibilities. For example, during finals week, she created a study schedule that broke down her subjects into manageable sections, just as she had done with her craft projects.

When she headed off to college, Emily was prepared. She knew how to balance her coursework, work commitments, and social life. Her peers often remarked on her exceptional time management skills, and she found herself in leadership roles within group projects because she understood the value of teamwork and accountability.

The Impact: Lifelong Lessons

Emily's journey illustrates how the small tasks instilled in her early years had a ripple effect throughout her life. By learning to take responsibility for her craft bin, she developed essential skills like organization, time management, and perseverance. These traits became ingrained in her identity, enabling her to navigate the challenges of adolescence and adulthood with confidence. Today, as a successful young professional, Emily reflects on her childhood experiences with gratitude. She recognizes that the habits she formed early on not only shaped her approach to responsibilities but also equipped her to handle challenges effectively.

Emily's story is a testament to the profound impact of early habit formation and the lifelong benefits of instilling responsibility in children.

The Long-Term Impact of Early Habit Formation
The habits children form in their early years do more than
just help them navigate childhood—they shape their entire
approach to responsibility, work ethic, and resilience as
adults. When kids are equipped with the tools to manage
tasks, solve problems, and take ownership of their actions,
they carry these valuable lessons into adulthood.
Consider adults who struggle with responsibility. Often, they
lack foundational skills that allow them to manage
commitments effectively. By instilling positive habits early,
parents can help prevent these challenges, ensuring their
children grow into responsible, capable adults.

Practical Tips

Encourage Problem-Solving: When children face challenges, guide them in figuring out solutions. This not only develops critical thinking skills but also reinforces the habit of persevering through difficulties.

Create a Routine: Children are more likely to form habits when tasks are part of a daily routine. Whether it's making their bed each morning or helping with dinner preparations, consistent repetition helps solidify these actions as automatic.

Model Desired Behaviour: Children are keen observers. If they see you demonstrating responsibility—whether through completing tasks on time or following through on commitments—they're likely to mimic that behaviour.

Conclusion:

As we wrap up this chapter, remember that forming positive habits is a journey, not a destination. It requires patience, consistency, and a willingness to adapt. By focusing on instilling responsibility through age-appropriate tasks, you are setting your children up for a lifetime of success.
Just like the path through the tall grass, each small step counts. And as your children grow, they'll navigate their own journeys with the skills and habits you've helped them cultivate. The foundation you lay now will guide them through challenges, instill resilience, and ultimately shape the adults they become.

So, embrace the messiness of the process and enjoy the little victories along the way. After all, every day is an opportunity to reinforce those habits that lead to responsible adulthood. As parents, you're the guiding force—leading them toward a future filled with promise, responsibility, and success.

Let's dig deeper now! There are quite a few reflection questions for this chapter. Please take time to really think about them and reflect on how you can create the environment you desire.

Reflection

What are some habits you developed during childhood that continue to influence your responsibilities today?
Can you identify both positive and negative habits?

Observation of Children:
Reflect on your child's daily routines. What habits do you notice? How do these habits align with the responsibilities you hope to instill in them?

Habit Formation Techniques:
Which habit formation techniques mentioned in the chapter do you think would be most effective for your child? Why?

Role of Environment:
How does your home environment support or hinder the formation of good habits in your children? What changes could you make to encourage positive habits?

Long-Term Goals:
What steps can you take now to guide them in developing habits that will support those long-term responsibilities?

Modelling Behaviour:
Reflect on your own habits. Are you modelling the behaviours you want your children to adopt?

Challenges and Solutions:
What challenges have you faced in helping your child develop good habits?

Celebrating Success:
How do you plan to celebrate your child's successes in habit formation? Why is it important to acknowledge their efforts along the way?

Notes:

Chapter 9

Bringing Your Family Values Into Every Task

As parents, the values we hold close—kindness, responsibility, respect—are woven into the fabric of our family life. We often think about teaching these values through big conversations or major life lessons, but the truth is that the everyday tasks we complete around the house are just as powerful. Whether it's cleaning up after dinner, doing laundry, or organizing family time, these small moments offer a unique opportunity to pass on what matters most to us.

Why Values Matter in Daily Routines

It might seem like chores are just a matter of keeping the household running smoothly, but in reality, they provide a consistent framework for teaching responsibility, empathy, and perseverance. Research suggests that children learn best when values are integrated into daily practices rather than through lectures or one-time conversations (Grusec & Goodnow, 1994). When we model our values during everyday tasks, we're creating a living example for our children to follow.

Think about something as simple as sharing. In a household where sharing is a key value, this could be seen in the way everyone contributes to the communal spaces. Maybe after dinner, everyone pitches in to clean up—whether it's clearing the table, washing the dishes, or wiping down counters. These actions may seem small, but the underlying message is: "We all contribute because we care about each other and our shared home." Over time, children internalize these lessons, learning that responsibility and teamwork are part of how we care for those we love.

Blending Cultural and Family Traditions Into Household Tasks

One of the most beautiful ways to teach family values is through cultural or family traditions. These rituals and routines can transform everyday tasks into something meaningful, connecting your children to their roots and teaching them important lessons about identity, pride, and continuity.

Household responsibilities aren't just about getting things done—they're a way to carry on traditions and culture, passing down what matters most to you. For some families, that might mean incorporating tasks like preparing traditional meals together. Imagine a family whose roots are in Italy. Every Sunday, they gather to make homemade pasta. The parents don't just teach the steps—they share stories about their grandparents doing the same, connecting their children to their heritage. By involving the kids in this task, they're not just teaching them how to cook; they're teaching the value of family, continuity, and pride in their roots.

> *We all contribute because we care about each other and our shared home.*

A family with Irish heritage might celebrate St. Patrick's Day by making a traditional Irish stew together and sharing stories about their ancestors. The process of cooking together becomes a way of passing down not just the recipe but also the values of family, perseverance, and heritage. By turning ordinary tasks into a reflection of cultural and family values, you're not just getting things done—you're creating a rich, shared experience that reinforces the importance of family traditions.

Tips for Blending Culture Into Household Tasks:
- Choose one traditional meal or activity that reflects your family's heritage and make it a regular part of your household routine.
- Use family tasks, like preparing for a holiday or event, as an opportunity to share stories about your culture or traditions with your children.
- Encourage your children to ask questions about why certain tasks are important to your family or culture, sparking meaningful conversations.

Instilling Core Values Through Routine Activities
Household tasks can teach a wide variety of values, depending on how they are framed. Here's how to use every day responsibilities to pass down the core values that shape your family life:

1. Responsibility and Accountability: Assigning age-appropriate chores to your children is one of the most straightforward ways to teach responsibility. When children learn that their actions (or lack thereof) have real consequences—like no clean clothes to wear or a messy room that's hard to play in—they start to understand the importance of being accountable. Giving them ownership of specific tasks, like feeding the family pet or organizing their toys, reinforces that they play a vital role in the family's daily operations.

You can emphasize this lesson by linking their contributions to the well-being of the whole family. For example, "When you help with the laundry, it means we all have clean clothes to wear, and that makes everyone feel good." Framing tasks this way helps them see how their actions have a positive impact on the family.

2. Empathy and Care for Others Simple tasks, like setting the table or making someone else's bed, can be a great way to teach children about empathy. Encourage your child to think about how their actions help others feel cared for and appreciated. You might say, "When you set the table, it makes dinnertime easier for everyone. It shows you care about us and helps us all enjoy our meal together." Another approach is to assign tasks that involve taking care of a sibling's needs. For instance, ask your older child to help pack a lunch for their younger sibling or have them assist in picking out an outfit for a family outing. These tasks nurture their ability to think beyond themselves, fostering a sense of empathy and care.

3. Perseverance and Hard Work Some household tasks are tough—whether it's scrubbing the bathroom or organizing a cluttered playroom. These harder chores are an excellent opportunity to teach perseverance. You can talk to your children about how not every task is fun, but finishing it feels rewarding. Share your own experiences, like how you push through tasks you don't enjoy because they lead to a better outcome.

In Real Life:

In the Patel household, chores weren't just tasks to get done—they were an opportunity to instill family values. Raj and Priya, parents to 10-year-old Ayesha and 7-year-old Neel, always believed that how their children approached responsibilities around the house would shape their character. So, instead of simply assigning chores, they used them as a way to reinforce the core values that were most important to their family: kindness, responsibility, and respect.

But this mindset hadn't always been easy. Like most kids, Ayesha and Neel would sometimes resist or try to rush through their chores just to get them done. It was then that Raj and Priya decided to make a change in how they framed household tasks, ensuring that every chore connected back to their family's core values.

Step 1: Connecting Responsibility to Family Pride
One evening, after dinner, Raj asked Ayesha and Neel to help clean up the kitchen. Ayesha groaned, as she usually did when it was her turn to wipe the counters, and Neel stalled by getting lost in his toy cars.

Priya noticed the growing tension and decided to take a different approach. She gently sat both kids down and said, "In our family, we take pride in taking care of each other. When we help clean up, we're not just doing a chore. We're showing that we care about our home and respect each other's space."

The kids listened, their attention drawn to how Priya connected a simple task to something bigger—their shared values. "So, when you clean the counters or help with the dishes, you're doing more than a chore. You're showing responsibility and respect for our family and our environment we all need to live in."

Step 2: Kindness in Every Action

The following weekend, it was time to clean the living room. Raj used this as an opportunity to talk about another key family value: kindness. "Neel, when we put away our toys and tidy up the living room, we're showing kindness to each other. We're making sure the space is nice for everyone."

He also mentioned how tidying up was a way of showing kindness to themselves. "When we come into a clean room, we feel calm and happy, right?" Neel nodded. He hadn't thought about cleaning as a way to be kind to himself and others, but it made sense. Tidying up wasn't just about the task—it was about creating a space where everyone could feel relaxed and comfortable.

Raj invited Neel to pick up the toys with him, reinforcing that they were working together as a team, and with each action, they were making their home a kinder place to live in.

Step 3: Respect for Others' Efforts

One day, Priya noticed that Ayesha had folded the laundry but left it in a pile on the couch. Instead of getting frustrated, Priya saw this as an opportunity to teach about respect—another important value in their family.

She called Ayesha over and said, "I see that you folded the clothes, which is great! But leaving them here for someone else to put away means they have to finish the job you started. In our family, respect means following through and not expecting others to complete what we leave unfinished."

Ayesha hadn't considered that leaving the laundry on the couch was disrespectful, but hearing it framed this way helped her understand the impact of her actions. She immediately picked up the laundry and took it to each family member's room, proud that she was showing respect for her parents' and brother's efforts.

Step 4: Using Chores to Build Stronger Family Bonds
Raj and Priya also wanted to make sure the kids understood that chores weren't just about keeping the house in order—they were a way for the family to stay connected and support each other.

One Saturday morning, they introduced a new tradition: "Family Clean-Up Hour." During this time, they would all tackle tasks together, sharing the work and talking as they went. Neel and Ayesha loved that it became a bonding experience. Whether it was sweeping the floor or organizing books, the family treated it as time spent together rather than just a series of chores.

Raj reinforced that working together as a team demonstrated another one of their core values—support. "When we all pitch in, we're supporting each other, just like we do in other parts of life."

For the Patel family, chores became more than just tasks—they became a way to bring their values into daily life. By connecting household responsibilities to kindness, responsibility, respect, and support, Raj and Priya helped Ayesha and Neel see that the work they did at home was a reflection of the people they were becoming.

Through their actions, the Patels showed that when chores align with core values, they not only get done but also build character. Each task became an opportunity for Ayesha and Neel to practice the qualities their parents wanted to nurture—turning everyday chores into life lessons that would stay with them far beyond childhood.

Practical Tips:

Eye Contact in Communication: Encourage your child to look you in the eyes when talking. It helps them focus, shows respect, and ensures they are paying attention to the conversation.

Get Down to Their Level: When communicating with young children, crouch down to their height. This makes them feel heard, respected, and more comfortable during interactions.

Ask for Repetition: After giving instructions, ask your child to repeat what you said. This ensures they've understood and gives you a chance to clarify if needed.

Conclusion:

Incorporating family values into daily tasks transforms chores into powerful lessons in responsibility, empathy, and perseverance. By modelling these values consistently, we help our children understand that contributing to the family is both important and rewarding. Blending cultural traditions into these activities enriches their understanding of heritage and pride. Ultimately, these moments of shared responsibility foster a sense of belonging and teamwork, shaping our children's character for years to come.

Reflection Questions

How can you better align your family's everyday routines with the values you want to teach your children?

What tasks could you turn into rituals that reflect your family's culture or traditions?

Notes:

"*Fathers, don't stir up anger in your children, but bring them up in the training and instruction of the Lord.*" *Eph.6:4 (NKJV)*

Chapter 10

The Lifelong Benefits of Instilling Responsibility

We often focus on the here and now—how to get our children to help out around the house, develop good habits, and manage their schoolwork. But the lessons we teach through everyday tasks go far beyond childhood. These simple chores, which may feel small or even mundane, are the building blocks for essential life skills that carry into adulthood. From responsibility to perseverance, the traits cultivated early on shape who our children will become and how they navigate the world.

From Chores to Life Skills

Consider how simple tasks like tidying up, doing laundry, or taking out the trash evolve as children grow. Initially, these responsibilities teach basic skills, but as time goes on, they lay the foundation for something much greater: the ability to manage their time, set goals, and stay accountable to themselves and others.

Think about an adult who learned responsibility early. They'll be the ones who meet work deadlines, manage a household smoothly, and approach challenges with resilience. Psychology shows us that individuals who develop a sense of responsibility early are more likely to experience success in their professional and personal lives. Dr. Angela Duckworth, author of Grit, emphasizes how perseverance, built through consistent efforts over time, is one of the key predictors of success. The small but steady responsibilities given to children allow them to develop this grit—a trait that will serve them in their careers and relationships for decades to come.

Let's take Alex, now 25, who started helping with household budgeting as a teen. Today, as a young professional managing his own finances, he handles budgeting and planning with ease. This confidence comes from years of practice, beginning with the small steps of balancing allowances and managing his own spending. Those early lessons? They created an adult who is financially literate, organized, and prepared for the complexities of adult life.

How Responsibility Translates to Adulthood Success
As children grow, the sense of responsibility they develop becomes a key driver in adulthood. When kids are trusted with tasks, they learn accountability—not just to parents or teachers but to themselves. That inner accountability translates into work ethic and self-discipline as adults. Sociological studies show that children who regularly contribute to family tasks are more likely to feel a sense of belonging and competence. This feeling extends into their work environments, making them more adaptable and cooperative team members (Grusec & Davidov, 2010).

When they become adults, these individuals are the ones who can be trusted with complex tasks, deadlines, and leadership roles. Responsibility becomes an intrinsic part of who they are. It's not just about taking care of tasks; it's about the ability to be relied upon—whether by colleagues, family members, or friends.

Resilience Through Challenges

One of the greatest benefits of giving children responsibility is the way it teaches resilience. Every challenge they overcome, from solving a tricky math problem to managing their tasks, builds a little more strength. As adults, they're less likely to be thrown off course by setbacks because they've learned how to handle difficulties from an early age.

Research in psychology supports this. Carol Dweck's work on growth mindset highlights the importance of teaching children that effort leads to improvement. When kids approach tasks with this mindset, they come to see challenges not as roadblocks but as opportunities to grow. By fostering resilience early, we help them develop a mental toughness that will help them push through difficult times later in life.

Sarah, a 30-year-old marketing executive, often reflects on the chores her parents assigned her growing up. While cleaning the garage wasn't glamorous, she learned the value of sticking to a task until it was finished. Today, when Sarah faces high-pressure projects at work, she draws on that same resilience to meet deadlines and push through challenges—knowing she can handle whatever comes her way.

Strong Relationships Rooted in Teamwork

One of the more understated but equally important lessons learned through childhood responsibilities is the value of teamwork. Sharing the load with family members teaches children that life isn't meant to be handled alone. As adults, they'll carry this understanding into their friendships, work relationships, and partnerships.

From a sociological perspective, household tasks help children internalize cooperation and empathy. They learn that contributing to the family's well-being is not only a responsibility but a way of showing care and respect for others. This cooperative spirit stays with them as they form their own communities in adulthood.

Imagine Sophia, now 28, who grew up helping her parents care for younger siblings and manage family meals. Today, as she navigates her career, she excels in team environments, offering support and working well with others. The social skills she honed as a child—patience, compromise, and empathy—have become key strengths in her personal and professional life.

The Ripple Effect: From Family to Community
The responsibilities children learn at home ripple out into the wider world. Adults who were given responsibilities early on tend to be more engaged in their communities. Whether they're volunteering, mentoring others, or contributing to a team at work, they've developed a mindset that seeks to make a difference.

Sociological studies show that individuals who grew up with a sense of duty within their families are more likely to participate in civic duties like voting, volunteering, and community service (McHale et al., 2000).

Practical Tips

Encourage Self-Reflection: Help your child look back on their experiences with chores and responsibilities. Ask them how they've seen these skills benefit them in school, friendships, or hobbies. This reflective process helps them internalize the value of their work.

Model Problem-Solving in Real-Life Scenarios: Share with your child how you tackle challenges in your work or household management. Let them see how the same skills they've developed—like perseverance and teamwork—are essential for adult success.

Link Chores to Bigger Life Goals: Talk to your child about how their contributions to the family prepare them for larger goals, such as managing their own home or balancing work-life responsibilities. This connects everyday tasks to their future ambitions.

Conclusion:

Instilling responsibility in our children equips them with invaluable life skills that extend far beyond the household. The lessons learned through everyday tasks—like time management, resilience, and teamwork—become essential tools for navigating adulthood. As they learn to care for others and understand the value of hard work, they grow into capable individuals ready to face life's challenges with confidence. Each chore completed is not just a task; it's a stepping stone toward a future filled with purpose and connection. By nurturing these qualities, we empower our children to thrive personally and professionally, setting the stage for a fulfilling and successful life.

Reflection Questions

How can I support my child in using the lessons from their tasks to tackle larger challenges in school, friendships, and future careers?

Do I take the time to self-reflect?

How am I doing this week? Have I made notable changes and progress to changing the way I do things?

Notes:

Chapter 11

Chores aka Tasks, That Strengthen Family Bonds and Build Character

Chores have long been seen as essential for maintaining a tidy home, but they serve a far greater purpose. When done together as a family, chores become opportunities for bonding, learning responsibility, and building character. Instilling responsibility early through shared household tasks not only helps children develop essential life skills but also fosters a deeper sense of connection between family members.

The Lifelong Benefits of Instilling Responsibility Early

When children are given age-appropriate tasks, they begin to understand the value of contributing to the family unit. These early experiences shape how they view responsibility and accountability throughout their lives. Studies have shown that children who take on household responsibilities from a young age are more likely to develop self-discipline, work ethic, and independence as they grow older (Rossmann, 2002).

The key is starting small and gradually increasing the level of responsibility as they mature. A toddler helping to put away toys might seem like a simple task, but it teaches them that their actions matter. As they grow, they can take on more complex tasks, like washing dishes or helping prepare meals, which further reinforces the sense of accomplishment and pride that comes from a job well done. By encouraging responsibility early, parents are setting their children up for success in adulthood. Whether in school, work, or personal relationships, the ability to manage tasks, take ownership, and follow through are skills that will serve them well in every aspect of life.

How Shared Chores Create Deeper Connections Between Family Members

Chores aren't just about getting things done—they can also be a powerful tool for strengthening family bonds. When everyone in the household shares in the work, it fosters a sense of teamwork and collaboration. Rather than seeing chores as burdens, children can learn that these tasks are part of contributing to the well-being of the family as a whole.

Imagine a family cleaning up after dinner together. While one child wipes down the table, another helps load the dishwasher, and a parent sweeps the floor. In this moment, everyone is working toward a common goal, and there's a sense of unity that comes from shared effort. This collaborative environment helps children understand that they are an integral part of the family and that their contributions matter.

Moreover, shared chores provide opportunities for meaningful conversations. Whether it's folding laundry together or preparing meals, these moments of routine work often open the door to discussions about school, friendships, or even dreams for the future. It's in these everyday moments that family members learn more about each other, creating deeper connections that go beyond the tasks at hand.

Raising Resilient Kids Who Understand the Value of Hard Work

Resilience is one of the most important traits we can cultivate in our children, and chores are an excellent way to teach this quality. Not every task will be easy or enjoyable, but by persevering through challenges, children learn the value of hard work and develop a strong sense of determination.

For example, a child who is tasked with cleaning a messy room might initially feel overwhelmed. However, by breaking the task down into smaller steps and sticking with it, they learn how to tackle problems head-on, even when the work seems difficult. This builds a mindset of persistence, which is critical in helping children develop resilience.
Hard work also teaches children that rewards often come after effort. The satisfaction of seeing a clean room or the praise from a parent after completing a chore provides positive reinforcement for their efforts. Over time, they begin to internalize the value of working toward goals, even when the process is challenging. This understanding of effort and reward will translate into other areas of life, from academics to personal relationships.

Practical Tips:

Teach Self-Discipline

Help your child learn to manage their time and impulses by setting clear expectations and routines. Let them experience natural consequences when they procrastinate or avoid tasks, so they understand the importance of following through.

Foster Gratitude

Encourage a sense of gratitude by regularly discussing what your family is thankful for. You can make this part of your dinner conversation or bedtime routine. When kids learn to appreciate what they have, they become more compassionate and generous.

Encourage Open Communication

Create an environment where your child feels comfortable sharing their thoughts and feelings without judgment. This teaches them the value of honesty and helps them develop emotional intelligence as they navigate social relationships.

Teach Accountability and Apologizing

Mistakes are opportunities for growth. When your child does something wrong, guide them through making amends and taking responsibility. Help them understand the importance of a sincere apology and how it can strengthen relationships.

Conclusion

Cultivating character growth in your child is a journey that requires patience, consistency, and intentionality. By modelling positive behaviours, encouraging empathy, and giving them responsibilities that grow with them, you are laying the foundation for a lifetime of integrity, resilience, and compassion. These values not only shape who they become as individuals but also how they contribute to their communities and navigate the challenges of adulthood. As parents, the lessons we teach today will empower our children to thrive tomorrow.

Reflection Questions

Do I look at chores, aka tasks, differently now than when I started this book?

What elements will I or have I implemented in my life?

What actions am I going to take to keep up with the changes?

Notes:

____

____

____

____

____

____

____

____

____

____

____

____

____

____

"Train up a child in the way he should go, and when he is old he will not depart from it." – Proverbs 22:6 (NKJV)

Final Thoughts

A Journey of Growth, Connection, and Character

As you've made your way through these pages, I hope you've seen how something as simple as household tasks can have such a profound impact on your child's growth and your family's connection. The tasks your children do today aren't just about keeping a clean house or completing a checklist—they're shaping their character, teaching them responsibility, and giving them tools for life.

You're not just raising helpers, you are raising capable, confident, and resilient individuals. Each time your child picks up a broom, sets the table, or waters the plants, they're building the habits and values that will carry them into adulthood. And the best part? You're doing it together, side by side, strengthening your family bond with every shared moment.

I want to remind you that it's okay to have days where the house is a mess, and it feels like nothing's getting done. Parenting isn't about perfection; it's about progress. You're laying the foundation, one task at a time, for a future where your children will thrive.

So keep going! Keep encouraging your kids, keep modelling hard work, and keep nurturing that sense of responsibility in your home. Each small task is a step toward building character, and each shared responsibility brings you closer as a family. You've got this! You're raising strong, capable kids who are ready for whatever life throws their way. And that's something to celebrate.

Remember: this isn't just about doing tasks; it's about shaping lives.

If you enjoyed this book, I would kindly ask if you could leave a review so more parents will be able to access this valuable information, as Amazon's algorithm will present it to more people as the review count increases.

Again, thank you for choosing "Raising Capable Kids: The Ultimate Guide to Tasks, Character, & Confidence."

**If you have enjoyed this book,
please consider leaving a review and letting others
know how this book has changed your home!**

Age-Appropriate Task Cheat Sheet

Ages 2-3
- Put toys back in their designated spots
- Help dust furniture with a cloth
- Put napkins or utensils on the table
- Place dirty clothes in the hamper
- Help water indoor plants
- Put books back on a shelf
- Wipe down surfaces with a damp cloth (e.g., table after meals)
- Throw away trash (like a tissue or small piece of paper)
- Push in chairs after meals
- Help wipe up small spills with supervision

Ages 4-5
- Make their bed with some assistance
- Feed pets with supervision
- Help clear the table after meals
- Help sort clean laundry into piles (socks, shirts, etc.)
- Match socks when folding laundry
- Help load the washing machine (with guidance)
- Wipe down kitchen counters
- Pull weeds in the garden (with supervision)
- Help carry groceries from the car to the house
- Put their toys or books away in the proper bins or shelves

Ages 6-7

- Make their bed neatly on their own
- Set and clear the table
- Empty small trash cans
- Fold simple items of laundry (towels, shirts)
- Help put away groceries
- Sort laundry by colors
- Clean windows with a spray bottle (light supervision)
- Help prepare simple breakfast items (toast, cereal)
- Empty small bathroom trash cans
- Put groceries away in the pantry or fridge

Ages 8-9

- Take out the trash
- Fold and put away their laundry
- Load and unload the dishwasher
- Sweep the floors
- Help prepare simple meals (with supervision)
- Make their own school lunch (with supervision)
- Clean up after pets (feed, water, tidy up pet areas)
- Organize the refrigerator or pantry
- Sweep the kitchen or entryways
- Help with meal prep by chopping soft vegetables or measuring ingredients

Ages 10-12

- Vacuum and mop floors
- Take full responsibility for their own laundry
- Clean the bathroom (sink, mirror, toilet)
- Rake leaves or shovel snow
- Wash dishes or load the dishwasher independently
- Change bed sheets and pillowcases
- Walk the family dog (with supervision if needed)
- Wash the family car (with guidance)
- Clean out and organize their school backpack or desk
- Sweep the garage or patio area
- **Ages 13-15**
- Mow the lawn or do other yard work
- Babysit younger siblings (with guidance)
- Cook a simple meal without assistance
- Clean and organize common areas of the house
- Manage personal hygiene routines independently
- Deep clean the kitchen (wipe cabinets, mop floor)
- Take over meal planning for a day (plan, shop, and cook)
- Wash windows or clean outdoor furniture
- Teach younger siblings how to do certain chores
- Manage household recycling (sort, take out)

Ages 15-18

- **Cook full meals independently** – Plan, prepare, and clean up after cooking dinner for the family.

- **Manage personal finances** – Create and stick to a budget, manage savings, and handle small bills (e.g., phone).

- **Take responsibility for scheduling** – Manage personal and family appointments or activities (with reminders).

- **Grocery shopping** – Make a list, shop for groceries, and stay within a budget.

- **Deep clean the house** – Scrub bathrooms, vacuum/mop floors, and clean windows or mirrors.

- **Laundry for the whole household** – Wash, dry, fold, and distribute laundry for all family members.

- **Yard work or gardening** – Mow the lawn, weed, plant flowers, or help maintain garden beds.

- **Home maintenance tasks** – Help with minor repairs, paint rooms, or assemble furniture.

- **Drive siblings to and from activities** (with a valid license) – Assist with transportation and time management.

- **Organize storage areas** – Declutter and organize the garage, attic, or closets.

About the Author

Faith Rachelle has dedicated 20 years to the Early Childhood Education field, offering her professional expertise and personal insights into child development. With extensive training and hands-on experience, she brings a deep understanding of how children function from both a psychological and practical perspective. Faith's work has ranged from managing classrooms of up to 20 energetic preschoolers to providing individualized tutoring for elementary

students, helping to guide young minds at every stage. Additionally, she has successfully coached parents through behavioural challenges in their children. Faith now focuses on writing books and teaching courses that empower parents and children to thrive.

"To every parent who picked up this book, thank you. Your dedication to raising respectful, capable, and compassionate children inspires me deeply. Writing this book was a labour of love, with the hope that the lessons shared will make your parenting journey a little easier and more rewarding. Your commitment to guiding the next generation with care and patience is the foundation of a brighter future. From my heart to yours—thank you for allowing me to be part of your family's story."

With gratitude,
Faith Rachelle

Reviews

Emily Peters

Toronto, Canada

"This book completely transformed how I approach parenting. It gave me practical, age-appropriate ideas for chores that actually work, and the insights on building responsibility and self-confidence in kids are invaluable. My children are more helpful and engaged, and I can already see the positive changes in their behaviour and self-esteem. A must-read for every parent looking to raise responsible, confident children!"

Thompson Family

British Columbia, Canada

"Finally, a parenting book that provides real solutions! I've always struggled with motivating my kids to do chores, but this book made it so much easier. The emphasis on teaching core values like empathy and teamwork through everyday tasks really resonated with me. I highly recommend this book to any parent who wants to foster lifelong values in their children while also creating a more harmonious household."

Sophia M.

Washington, USA

"This book is a game-changer for families! The chore systems are simple yet incredibly effective, and the emotional benefits—like building stronger family connections—are worth every minute spent following the advice. I love how the author blends cultural and family traditions into the chores, making them meaningful beyond just tasks. This book doesn't just give you tips, it helps you raise kind, responsible kids who understand the value of hard work."

Candice Halmic

Alberta, Canada

"I've read many parenting books, but this one stands out for its actionable advice and the way it teaches children responsibility without feeling like you're nagging them. The section on fostering pride and ownership through chores was an eye-opener for me. I started implementing the strategies with my kids, and I've already seen a huge shift in their attitude toward helping out around the house. This book is a must-read for any parent!"

Jody Desmin

Arizona, USA

"As a parent of three, I've always struggled with getting my kids to do chores without constant reminders. This book provided a clear, easy-to-follow system that made chores feel less like a battle and more like a family activity. The emotional growth I've seen in my kids—from teamwork to developing a strong work ethic—has been incredible. This book is packed with wisdom and practical tools for building a stronger, more responsible family."

References

All the scriptures:

Holy Bible. (1982). NKJV. Thomas Nelson.
Luke 16:10, Prov.22:6, Colossians 3:23, Eccl. 9:10, Phili. 4:8, Ps.133:1, Eph. 4:32, Eph. 6:4, Heb 10:24

Lythcott-Haims, J. (2016). How to raise an adult: Break free of the overparenting trap and prepare your kid for success — S — Martin'ss Griffin.

Rossmann, M. M. (2014). The impact of household chores on children's success. *Journal of Developmental Psychology.*

Taylor, J. (2011). *Your children are listening: Nine messages they need to hear from you.* Workman Publishing.

Golinkoff, R. M., & Hirsh-Pasek, K. (2016). *Becoming Brilliant: What science tells us about raising successful children.* American Psychological Association.

American Academy of Pediatrics. (n.d.). Developmentally appropriate chores for children.

Berridge, K. C., & Kringelbach, M. L. (2015). Pleasure systems in the brain. *Neuron, 86*(3), 646–664. https://doi.org/10.1016/j.neuron.2015.02.018

Carter, C. S. (2014). Oxytocin pathways and the evolution of human behaviour. *Annual Review of Psychology, pp. 65,* 17–39. https://doi.org/10.1146/annurev-psych-010213-115110

Rizzolatti, G., & Craighero, L. (2004). The mirror-neuron system. *Annual Review of Neuroscience, 27,* 169–192. https://doi.org/10.1146/annurev.neuro.27.070203.144230

Dweck, C. S. (2006). *Mindset: The new psychology of success*. Random House.

Deci, E. L., & Ryan, R. M. (2000). The "what" and "why" of goal pursuits: Human needs and the self-determination of behaviour. *Psychological Inquiry, 11*(4), 227–268.

Diamond, A. (2013). Executive functions. *Annual Review of Psychology, pp. 64,*–135–168.

Grusec, J. E., & Goodnow, J. J. (1994). Impact of parental discipline methods on the child's internalization of values: A reconceptualization of current points of view. *Developmental Psychology, 30*(1), 4-19.

Skinner, B. F. (1938). *The behaviour of organisms: An experimental analysis*. Appleton-Century.

Whiting, B. B., & Edwards, C. P. (1988). *Children of different worlds: The formation of social behaviour*. Harvard University Press.

Bandura, A. (1977). *Social learning theory*. Prentice-Hall.

Bronson, P., & Merryman, A. (2009). *NurtureShock: New thinking about children*. Twelve.

Vygotsky, L. S. (1978). *Mind in society: The development of higher psychological processes*. Harvard University Press.

Bear, G. G., & Watkins, J. M. (2006). Promoting moral development in schools. *Journal of Moral Education, 35*(2),–169–183.

Grusec, J. E., & Hastings, P. D. (Eds.). (2015). *Handbook of socialization: Theory and research* (2nd ed.). Guilford Press.

Grusec, J. E., & Davidov, M. (2010). Socialization in the family: The roles of parents. In M. H. Bornstein (Ed.), *The handbook of life-span development*.

McHale, S. M., Crouter, A. C., & Tucker, C. J. (2000). Family context and gender role socialization in middle childhood: Comparing girls to boys. *Child Development, 71*(4), 990–1004.

Duckworth, A. (2016). *Grit: The power of passion and perseverance*. Scribner.

Conestoga Driving Schools | Kitchener Waterloo Driving Schools - Kitchener Waterloo Cambridge Guelph Driving Schools. http://www.kwdrivingschools.com/driving-school/4-Conestoga_Driving_School.htm

Building Resilience in Your Professional Life. https://www.pmtraining.com/about/building-resilience-in-your-professional-life

Duhigg, C. (2012). *The Power of Habit: Why We Do What We Do in Life and Business*. Random House.
Mischel, W. (2014). *The Marshmallow Test: Mastering Self-Control*. Little, Brown and Company.